THE CAMPFIRE COOKBOOK

THE CAMPFIRE COOKBOOK

80 imaginative recipes for cooking outdoors

VIOLA LEX
NICO STANITZOK

Off on new adventures!

If it's the sense of independence in particular that attracts you to camping, we know exactly how you feel. Camping is like a fusion of wanderlust and joie de vivre. It is pure freedom!

We like to think of ourselves as globetrotters, always on the move, trying to quench our insatiable desire to travel. It's a passion we share and that inspired us to create this cookbook. Travel has brought us such joy, and we want you to experience some of that, too. We'd like to accompany you on your trip with our book—full of useful tips and fine food.

We know from our own experiences that cooking outdoors has far more to offer than dried soup packets and canned ravioli. We have happy memories of childhood days at various campsites and also recall more daring exploits as adults. I, Nico, am at my most content when immersed in the natural world, and for Viola, bliss is a VW camper van (a T3 with the nickname "Lucy," which belongs to her sister). As backpackers, we've already trekked all over the globe. Viola has pitched her tent in the Colombian jungle, and at one point my desire for adventure grew so strong that I went off to live in Thailand.

All the things that really excite us about camping are here in this book. It's the ideal guide for your camping trip: it doesn't matter whether you are a large family or a solo festivalgoer, young or old, thrifty or spendthrift—the main thing is, you need to be hungry for the outside life!

We hope you really enjoy our camping cookbook.

Viola Lex & Nico Stanitzok

Which type of camper are you?

The camper van enthusiast

Free spirits feel totally at home in a retro camper van, and you will often see stylish surfing types traveling in them! A popular trip with camper van users is to potter leisurely cross-country around North America or New Zealand. Here's a typical schedule for a camper van enthusiast: sleep in, do a yoga session, go surfing, grab some rays, enjoy a beer.

The luxury camper

These campers don't like to be without their creature comforts on vacation, so they transform their motor homes into luxury oases on wheels, complete with a high-tech kitchen, washing machine, flat-screen TV, and even a garage—everything is on board! Or some prefer "glamping," which is currently all the rage, with camping accommodation provided in well-equipped and partially furnished luxury tents at glamorous sites.

The wilderness camper

"Back to your roots" is the motto for the inveterate wilderness camper. These genuine nature lovers are eager for adventure and like to hike, cook over a campfire, and camp out in the woods. Equipment—from underwear to cooking utensils—has to be functional for this kind of camper.

The family camper

Whether in a caravan or a tent, these campers are determined to take everything but the kitchen sink with them on their travels. Bicycles, windbreakers—you name it, you'll find it in their luggage. The "new parent" camper is also often seen on campsites. Newbie moms and dads are big fans of mobile accommodations for their first vacation with the baby.

The festival camper

Festivalgoers want one thing above all else: a party! A place to sleep merely serves as somewhere to chill out briefly between all the dancing. For these kinds of campers, everything needs to be uncomplicated and practical. After all, who wants to waste time setting up camp or cooking when you'd rather be partying?

The long-term camper

The long-term camper can be thought of as the campsite's indigenous inhabitant. These campers laboriously transform their plot into a second home, complete with tent and awning, kitchenette, and TV connection. They are both mocked and feared, but there's no need to be frightened of these unofficial "bosses": new arrivals are usually warmly welcomed by them.

Enjoy your vacation!

Once you've filled up the tank in the camper van or have gotten the tent ready for action, your trip can begin. You can call anywhere in the world home and decide on the spur of the moment where to spend the night. Relaxation is the order of the day! Traveling this way is addictive—and it works up an appetite! Despite having only a small kitchen, there's no need to miss out when you're camping—especially when it comes to the pleasure of eating, as we will reveal!

A camping trip requires good preparation, which is why even the most relaxed outdoor adventurers suddenly become avid list writers. However, there's no need to start fretting because we've taken charge of the planning so you can relax and simply pack. You'll find checklists for basic ingredients and kitchen equipment on p156. To make your life even easier, we have also provided great ideas for supplies on p12, camping stove tips on p66, and clever skills for the barbecue on p112—as well as lots of other survival tips for campers.

Relax

Vacations often start in the local supermarket where you can saunter around the aisles and discover what your vacation destination has to offer. Our cookbook is full of recipes to inspire you and help you enjoy the feeling of eating outdoors, in the fresh air, together and happy! Even if you have only a small camping kitchen, our recipes are guaranteed to succeed. They are amazingly delicious and easy to follow—from one-pot dishes to pan-cooked bread. Et voilà... the food is ready!

Camping kitchen secrets

The aim is to keep things simple, so anything you don't need should be left at home, such as the kitchen scales. For our recipes, you need only a tablespoon, teaspoon, or cup or favorite camping mug with a capacity of 9fl oz (250ml) for measuring. Where other measures are given, simply purchase the amount needed or use the measures on packaging to guide you. What else do you need to pack? This book, of course. We've had it made in a handy format for traveling so you'll always have plenty of camping recipes up your sleeve during your travels.

Get cooking

It doesn't matter if you are a solo camper, a couple, or a four-person family—to make sure everyone gets their fill, we've designed the recipes to feed four people. The only exception is if you are cooking with just one camping stove burner or if you're preparing one of our instant dishes, in which case the ingredients will be enough for two people. If you do end up with leftovers, you can look forward to finishing these off the following day. But wait and see—camping usually makes you very hungry, and you might have a spontaneous visit from your camping neighbors!

Useful symbols

The following symbols are used throughout the book to help you choose the most suitable recipes:

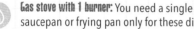

Road trip: Prepare these recipes before you set off. They are great for the outbound trip or for trips while away.

Cold dishes: These can be made without a gas stove or a barbecue.

Gas stove with 1 burner: You need a single saucepan or frying pan only for these dishes.

Gas stove with 2 burners: You will need to use two pans at the same time for these dishes.

Barbecue: These recipes are prepared on the barbecue grill.

Tips and information: Includes clever tips for recipes or general advice for campers.

All in the timing

We cook our recipes using a camping stove or barbecue, but every camper has his own personal preference, so our recipes also work with other types of equipment. It doesn't matter what equipment you choose; just remember that cooking times will vary. Factors that can affect cooking time include the specific equipment and fuel used as well as the temperature and altitude. The recipes in this book give approximate timings, so use these as a guideline only. Always test to make sure your food is cooked.

The mobile pantry

Space-saving solutions

Make sure your vacation time is dedicated to enjoying the finer things in life, not on wasting time hunting for basic ingredients. Before you set off, decant pasta and flour into rectangular storage containers, which are ideal for stacking when space is at a premium. You can also pack up sugar, stock, dishwashing liquid, and special ingredients such as capers in handy travel containers.

Camping kitchen essentials

If you want to travel with minimal luggage, you'll love these lightweight items. Resealable freezer bags are super versatile for outdoor cooking and eating. They can be used to store ready-made muesli mixtures for breakfast, power snacks for when you're on the move, marinades for meat, or portions of "instant" meals that just need rehydrating (see recipes, pp90–91). And when you're camping, you can't be without aluminum foil—an essential item.

Spice combos

Whether it's rosemary, cinnamon, or paprika, spices and herbs are crucial in a campsite kitchen. You can either buy spice boxes that can accommodate lots of little portions of different herbs or spice combinations, or just decant your favorites into empty containers—and don't forget to label them! Then you can enjoy discovering fresh herbs at local markets. And if you are really confident about identifying plants, you could collect wild herbs—where permitted.

Homemade condiments

Homemade food can't be beaten when it comes to taste—and the same is true for delicious homemade barbecue sauces. There's no need to dispense with the do-it-yourself trend for supplies when traveling. Smart campers prepare ketchup and barbecue sauces (see recipes, pp14–16) in their kitchen at home then take these along with them.

Versatile ingredients

It's worth planning your supplies well so that one ingredient can be used for several recipes. Pack some cocoa powder and use it to make Pan-Cooked Apple Cake (see p110) or Chocolate Cake (see p155) plus hot chocolate every morning for the kids. The same applies when shopping locally: for example, put a double portion of feta cheese into your shopping basket so you can cook Green Asparagus Salad (see p54) for lunch followed by Greek Pan-Cooked Pasta (see p80) for supper.

Thirst quenchers

Before you leave, freeze plastic bottles filled with tap water. This is a double bonus because you'll have drinking water on hand for the trip, plus while the bottles are defrosting in the cooler, any food stored alongside them will be kept cold. Remember, though, that water expands when it freezes. Pour a generous splash of water out of the bottles before freezing them.

Ketchup

2 tbsp canola oil
2 onions, diced
5 tbsp sugar
4 tbsp apple cider vinegar
2 tbsp applesauce
4 cups (2 x 14oz/400g cans) chopped
   tomatoes
½ tsp curry powder
salt

Also

2 screw-top bottles (16fl oz/500ml
   each), rinsed with hot water

1 Heat the oil in a pan. Sweat the onions in the hot oil over medium heat for 2 minutes. Add the sugar and sauté over low heat for another 6 minutes.

2 Add the vinegar to deglaze the pan then add the applesauce, tomatoes, and curry powder. Stir and simmer over medium heat for about 10 minutes, stirring occasionally to prevent the sauce from sticking to the pan. Finally, purée the mixture using a handheld blender and season to taste with salt. Pour into bottles through a funnel while it is still hot, and then seal. The sealed ketchup will keep unrefrigerated for up to a month. Once opened, refrigerate and use within 2 weeks.

Makes about 34 oz (1 liter) · preparation time about 35 minutes

Banana Ketchup

2 tbsp peanut oil
1 small onion, diced
2 garlic cloves, finely chopped or crushed
1 jalapeño chile, seeded and halved
1¾in (4cm) piece of ginger, peeled and
   grated
½ tsp ground turmeric
¼ tsp ground allspice
½ cup white wine vinegar
2 tbsp honey
2 tbsp dark rum
1 tbsp tomato purée
1 tbsp soy sauce
4 bananas
salt

Also
2 screw-top bottles (16fl oz/500ml each),
   rinsed with hot water

1 Heat the oil in a pan. Sweat the onion over medium heat for 5 minutes. Add the garlic, chile, ginger, turmeric, and allspice and sauté for 30 seconds. Add the vinegar to deglaze the pan, and then add the honey, rum, tomato purée, and soy sauce and stir until smooth. Peel the bananas, chop into rough pieces, and add to the pan. Cover with a lid and simmer over low heat for 15 minutes, stirring regularly. Remove the pan from the heat and let cool for 10 minutes.

2 Transfer the banana mixture to a food processor and purée well for about 1 minute, adding water as needed to produce the desired consistency. Alternatively, purée the mixture using a handheld blender.

3 Return the mixture to the pan and bring to a boil once more, stirring constantly. Season to taste with salt. Transfer into bottles while still boiling hot and seal immediately. The sealed ketchup will keep unrefrigerated for up to a month. Once opened, refrigerate and use within 2 weeks.

Family vacation trial run
If you're planning a family camping trip but your kids have never spent a night in a tent before, give them a trial run before you head off into the distance on your annual vacation. Go on a short weekend camping trip together first, or simply pitch your tent in the backyard for a night.

BBQ Sauce

1 tbsp canola oil
2 onions, diced
1 red pepper, seeded and diced
2 red chiles, seeded and quartered
14oz (400g) can peeled tomatoes
½ cup honey
1 tsp smoked salt, plus extra, to taste,
    and freshly ground black pepper
2 tbsp balsamic vinegar
1 tsp cornstarch

Also
2 screw-top bottles (10fl oz/ 300ml
    each), rinsed with hot water

1 Heat the oil in a pan. Sweat the onions, pepper, and chiles over medium heat for 5 minutes. Add the tomatoes, honey, and salt. Combine the vinegar and cornstarch, and stir into the mixture with a balloon whisk. Simmer everything for 10 minutes over medium heat, stirring occasionally.

2 Purée the thickened BBQ sauce with a handheld blender and season to taste with salt and pepper. Pour into the bottles while still hot, and seal. The sealed BBQ sauce will keep unrefrigerated for a month. Once opened, refrigerate and use within 2 weeks.

Smoked sophistication
Smoked salt is an aromatic salt that imbues dishes with a wonderful smoky flavor. This is a strong seasoning with an intense flavor, so be careful when you first add it, and taste everything again at the end.

For about 8 steaks or 2-3 flatbreads · preparation time about 20 minutes

Dukkah-Middle Eastern or African Spice Mixture

2 dried chiles
1¾oz (50g) roasted, salted peanuts, finely chopped
1¾oz (50g) hazelnuts, finely chopped
1¾oz (50g) pistachios, finely chopped
¾oz (20g) sesame seeds
3 tsp garlic granules
2 tsp ground cumin
2 tsp ground coriander
5 tsp fennel seeds
3 tsp coarse salt

1 Crush the chiles in a mortar or shred with your fingers. Toast the chiles, nuts, sesame seeds, garlic, spices, and salt in a dry pan over medium heat until they release their aroma.

2 Let cool then transfer to a freezer bag or screw-top jar to take with you on your trip.

Tastes fantastic with...
Try this mix with freshly baked flatbreads, dipped into olive oil and then into the dukkah mixture. Or toss some fish in dukkah before serving—we guarantee you'll experience aromatic pyrotechnics!

Apricot Cakes in a Jar

4 tbsp white bread crumbs
1½ cups dried apricots, finely diced
1½ cups all-purpose flour, plus
  1 tbsp
1 cup soft butter
1 cup sugar
juice of 2 oranges (about ½ cup) and
  zest of 1 orange
2–3 drops pure vanilla extract
4 eggs
½ cup cornstarch
2 tsp baking powder

Also
4 preserving jars with lids
  (16fl oz/500ml each)

1 Grease the jars and sprinkle 1 tablespoon of white bread crumbs into each. Make sure that the glass rim, which will later be in contact with the rubber seal, is left clear. Preheat the oven to 350°F (180°C). Combine the apricots with the 1 tablespoon of flour in a bowl.

2 Cream the butter with the sugar and the orange zest using an electric handheld blender. Add the orange juice and pure vanilla extract, and then gradually stir in the eggs one at a time, mixing for 30 seconds after each addition. Combine the 1½ cups of flour, cornstarch, and baking powder and add to the mix with the orange juice. Stir until combined, and then fold in the apricots.

3 Divide the mixture between the jars so they are about two-thirds full. Place in the center of the oven and bake for 35–40 minutes. Meanwhile, soak 4 rubber seals for the jars in water.

4 Remove the jars from the oven and place the rubber rings on the rim. Seal immediately with the lids and clip in place with the clasp. Let the cakes cool on a rack in the sealed jars. They will keep for about 2 weeks unopened and unrefrigerated. Tip them out of the jars to serve.

For 4 people or to store · preparation time about 10 minutes + soaking overnight

Camping Bircher Muesli Mixture

2 cups jumbo oats
4 tbsp hazelnuts, chopped
juice of 1 orange
½ cup milk
3½ oz (100g) cream cheese
1 cup low-fat yogurt plus 3½oz (100g)
2 tbsp honey
1 apple, finely diced or roughly grated

1 Combine the oats and hazelnuts in a bowl at home. Transfer to a small screw-top jar or freezer bag, seal, and take this with you, ready-prepared, on your trip.

2 Combine cream cheese with 3½ oz (100g) yogurt in a bowl. Stir the orange juice and milk together in a separate bowl. Add the cream cheese and yogurt mixture, the remaining yogurt, and honey, and stir everything until smoothly combined. Stir in the muesli mixture and leave to soak overnight in a fridge. Before serving, fold the apple into the muesli, and then divide the muesli between 4 bowls and serve.

Cranberry Muesli Bars

1 cup dried cranberries
4 tbsp butter
3 tbsp sugar
2 tbsp honey
1 tsp lemon juice
2 cups oats
⅓ cup chopped almonds
2 tbsp sunflower seeds

Also
parchment paper
baking dish (roughly 8 x 12in/20 × 30cm)

1 Line the baking dish with the parchment paper, and preheat the oven to 325°F (160°C). Finely chop the cranberries with a knife or blend them in the food processor.

2 Place the butter, sugar, honey, and lemon juice in a small pan and stir over medium heat until the sugar has completely dissolved. Combine the cranberries, oats, almonds, and sunflower seeds in a bowl. Carefully stir in the butter mixture, making sure everything is coated.

3 Transfer the mixture to the prepared baking dish, smooth the surface, and press it down slightly. Bake in the center of the oven for about 20 minutes.

4 Remove and let cool in the dish. Use the parchment paper to lift it out of the dish, and then slice into 12 bars.

On the road

Take it along with you

If you're eager to hit the road but find that typical truck-stop food is best avoided, just rustle up a couple of "snacks to go" while you're still at home (see recipes from p24). Our sandwiches are also ideal for day trips once you're at your vacation destination—whether you're off hiking in the mountains or enjoying a relaxing day at the beach.

Refueling

Do you need a quick burst of energy? Our supplies for the trip are perfect for a power break. While your vacation preparations are underway, get your oven working overtime to prepare Honey-Roasted Peanuts (see p30) or Cranberry Muesli Bars (see p21). These pick-me-up snacks will fit easily into your backpack in resealable freezer bags.

Pop it in a bag

Anyone who has ever eaten a sandwich on a road trip will recognize the scenario: no sooner do you take a bite from it than the tomato falls out onto the seat and the mayonnaise is in your lap. To prevent this, pack up your sandwiches in paper or plastic sandwich bags.

Shake it up

Using "salad shakers" makes life easier when you're on the move. These containers place the salad ingredients in one container and the dressing in a separate one, usually inside the lid, so the salad stays crisp and fresh. When you want to eat, just mix it all together. Shake it up!

A tight squeeze

Take a reusable drinking bottle with you on your trip. If you are scrambling for every last inch of space and watching every ounce of weight, it's worth acquiring a collapsible drinking bottle, which can be squeezed smaller when empty. And for anyone who is prone to getting cold feet: pour hot water into the bottle, wrap a T-shirt around it, and place it in your sleeping bag—now you have a homemade foot warmer.

Simple Crackers

2 cups all-purpose flour, plus extra
  for dusting
3 tsp baking powder
1 tbsp sugar
1 tsp salt, divided use
8 tbsp chilled butter, divided use
2 tbsp canola oil

Also
parchment paper
cookie cutters

1 Line 2 baking sheets with parchment paper. Preheat the oven to 400°F (200°C). Put the flour, baking powder, sugar, and ½ teaspoon of the salt in a bowl and mix well. Chop 4 tablespoons of the butter into pieces and add to the bowl. Knead everything together quickly with your hands. Add the oil and work into the mixture. Gradually add 3½ tablespoons of cold water and knead into a smooth dough.

2 Roll out the dough on a floured work surface to about ⅛in (3mm) thick. Cut out cracker shapes and place on the baking sheets. Prick each cracker with a fork. Place the sheets in the center of the oven, and bake the crackers for 12–14 minutes, until golden brown.

3 Melt the remaining butter and combine with the remaining salt. Remove the crackers from the oven and let cool. Brush with the melted salted butter while still hot.

Poppy Seed Crackers with Sesame

2½ cups all-purpose flour, plus extra
  for dusting
2 tbsp olive oil
salt
2 tbsp poppy seeds
1 tbsp sesame seeds
2 tbsp coarse sea salt

Also
plastic wrap
parchment paper

1 Use your hands to combine 1½ cups of the flour with ½ cup of water, the olive oil, and a pinch of salt in a bowl. Add the remaining flour and the poppy and sesame seeds, and knead everything by hand until you have a smooth dough. Wrap in plastic wrap and rest for 30 minutes.

2 Meanwhile, line 2 baking sheets with parchment paper. Preheat the oven to 425°F (220°C). Roll out the dough on a floured work surface to about ¼in (6mm) thick. Slice into 1½in (4cm) squares with a pastry wheel. Place the crackers on the baking sheets. Sprinkle with sea salt.

3 Put the sheets in the center of the oven, and bake the crackers for 12–15 minutes, until golden brown. Take the sheets out of the oven, use the paper to remove the crackers, and let cool on a wire rack.

For 4 people
Preparation time about 40 minutes

Mini Meatball Skewers

For the meatballs
½ bread roll
1 red onion, finely sliced
½ bunch of flat-leaf parsley, finely chopped
1lb 2oz (500g) ground beef
1 egg
1 tbsp white bread crumbs
1 tsp medium–hot mustard
1 tsp sweet paprika
1 tsp curry powder
salt and freshly ground black pepper
2 tbsp canola oil
16 cherry tomatoes
Gouda cheese, cut into 8 bite-sized cubes

Also
8 wooden skewers (6in/15cm each)

1 Soak the bread in hot water. Squeeze out the roll and place in a bowl with the onion, parsley, ground meat, egg, bread crumbs, mustard, paprika, and curry powder. Knead everything thoroughly with your hands until the mixture is well combined. Season to taste with salt and pepper and let rest for 10 minutes.

2 Shape 24 evenly sized balls from the meat mixture. Heat the oil in a pan. Fry the meatballs over medium heat for about 10 minutes until golden brown all over. Remove and drain on some paper towels, and let cool completely.

3 Meanwhile, wash the cherry tomatoes and leave to drain. Slide 3 meatballs, 2 cherry tomatoes, and a piece of cheese onto each skewer. Pack up into paper or plastic bags or put in an airtight container for your trip.

Two in one
Salt and pepper are crucial when cooking. For your camping kitchen, a functional piece of equipment for this spice duo is a dispenser that screws together from two sides so that each side can be filled with the separate condiments.

For 4 people
Preparation time about 20 minutes · infusion time about 24 hours

Layered Salad in a Jar

10oz (285g) can corn
8oz (235g) can pineapple pieces
3 celery sticks
2 eggs
3 tbsp mayonnaise
1 cup low-fat yogurt
salt and freshly ground black pepper
1 small leek, halved lengthwise, then cut
   into ⅛in (3mm) strips
¼ iceberg lettuce, thinly sliced
5½oz (150g) Gouda cheese, sliced into
   ¼in (6mm) strips
5½oz (150g) cooked ham, sliced into
   ¼in (6mm) strips

Also
4 screw-top jars (14fl oz/400ml each)

1 Strain the corn, pineapple, and celery in a colander and leave to drain. Cook the eggs in boiling water for 8 minutes then plunge them into cold water, peel, and let cool.

2 Combine the mayonnaise and yogurt in a bowl and season to taste with salt and pepper.

3 Layer all the ingredients except the cheese and eggs so they are evenly distributed in the jars, and drizzle with the mayonnaise dressing. Sprinkle with the cheese as the final layer. Chop the eggs into quarters and distribute between the jars. Seal the jars with the lids, and leave the salad in the fridge to infuse for about 24 hours.

For 4 people
Preparation about 25 minutes

Honey-Roasted Peanuts

1lb 2oz (500g) roasted, unsalted peanuts
1 cup honey
1 cup sugar
2 tsp salt

Also
parchment paper

1 Line a baking sheet with parchment paper. Preheat the oven to 350°F (180°C). Put the peanuts in a bowl. Heat the honey in a pan over medium heat until runny then pour the honey over the peanuts. Add the sugar and salt, and stir everything well until the peanuts are completely coated in honey and sugar.

2 Spread the peanuts evenly over the baking sheet, trying to make sure they aren't touching.

3 Place the sheet in the center of the oven and roast for about 15 minutes, turning the nuts halfway through. When the nuts are golden, remove and let cool completely on the sheet.

4 Break up the nut mixture with your fingers and then transfer to an airtight container or to a freezer or paper bag, ready for your hike or trip.

For 4 people · preparation time about 10 minutes

Papaya, Banana, and Nut Mix

5 tbsp banana chips
4 tbsp dried papaya, finely chopped
2 tbsp dried pineapple, finely chopped
1 cup whole almonds
1 cup cashews
5 tbsp pumpkin seeds
5 tbsp puffed quinoa
3 tbsp coconut flakes

1 Break the banana chips into small pieces. Mix all the ingredients in a bowl then pour into an airtight box. The nut mixture can also be transferred to a paper or freezer bag for your trip.

Old school

Remember the days before GPS and Google Maps? Even if it feels like taking a trip back in time, it's always advisable to take a trusty old road map with you. If your GPS or smartphone fail, the map will never let you down. Not to mention it's fun navigating yourself every now and then!

For 4 people · preparation time about 15 minutes · baking time about 30 minutes

Spiced Nuts with Pecorino Romano Cheese

2 cups roasted, unsalted pistachios,
  shells removed
1 cup whole almonds
2 cups walnuts
1 cup hazelnuts
2 tbsp honey
3 tbsp raw cane sugar
1 tsp smoked paprika
1 tsp ground cumin
½ tsp chili flakes
pinch of ground cinnamon
7oz (200g) Pecorino Romano cheese

Also
parchment paper

1 Mix together the pistachios, almonds, walnuts, and hazelnuts. Line a baking sheet with parchment paper. Preheat the oven to 300°F (150°C). Put the honey and sugar into a pan and bring to a boil over medium heat, stirring constantly. Once the sugar has dissolved, reduce the temperature and let the mixture simmer over low heat for another minute. Stir in the spices, add the nuts, and stir again until everything is covered with the honey mixture.

2 Spread the nuts evenly over the baking sheet, trying to make sure they aren't touching. Place the sheet in the center of the oven, and roast the nuts for 30 minutes. Turn them every 10 minutes, and then remove from the oven and let cool completely on the sheet.

3 Roughly grate the cheese. Break apart the nut mixture, combine with the cheese, and transfer to an airtight container.

For 4 people
Preparation time about 15 minutes · resting time 30 minutes

Mini Sandwich Rolls with Creamed Tuna

5oz (150g) can tuna
1 small onion, diced
3 tbsp mayonnaise
½ tsp dried basil
salt and freshly ground black pepper
8 slices of white sliced bread, crusts
    removed
¼ cucumber, peeled and quartered
    lengthwise

Also
2 pieces of plastic wrap (12 x 20in/
    30 × 50cm)

1 Drain the tuna in a colander. Put the drained tuna, onion, mayonnaise, and basil into a blender beaker and purée well using a handheld blender (see also tip, below). Season to taste with salt and pepper.

2 Roll out the slices of bread on the work surface with a rolling pin until they are as flat as possible. Spread the plastic wrap on a separate part of the work surface and place 2 slices of bread next to each other on it, so they overlap in the middle by about ½in (1cm). Spread the tuna mixture evenly over the slices of bread. Place 2 strips of cucumber on the lower edge of each one, and use the plastic wrap to help you roll up the slices of bread as tightly as possible. Repeat with the rest of the slices. Chill for about 30 minutes, and then unwrap and slice into ¾–1½in (2–4cm) thick rounds.

On a knife-edge
If you are preparing this recipe at home for your trip, you'll probably use a blender. In an improvised campsite kitchen, just chop everything very finely with a knife instead. Depending on the recipe you are preparing, if you have to manage without a blender, you can either press the ingredients using a fork or push them through a sieve.

Crispy Baguette with Turkey and Apricots

8 very thin turkey breasts (1¾oz/50g each,
   or 4 x 3½oz/100g steaks),
   pounded flat
salt and freshly ground black pepper
1 tbsp canola oil
8 slices bacon
1 cup soft apricots, finely chopped
1½in (4cm) piece of ginger, grated
1 red chile, seeded and finely chopped
2 tbsp honey
1 tsp mustard
1 tbsp white wine vinegar
4 tbsp mayonnaise
1 fresh baguette (about 20in/50cm long,
   3¼in/8cm diameter)
6 radicchio leaves, cut into very thin strips

1 Season the turkey breasts with salt and pepper. Heat the oil in a pan, and fry the breasts over high heat for 1 minute on each side. Take them out of the pan, leave to drain on paper towels, and set aside. In the same pan, fry the bacon on both sides until golden brown and crisp then set aside.

2 Combine the apricots, ginger, chile, honey, mustard, vinegar, and mayonnaise together in a bowl, and season to taste with salt and pepper.

3 Slice the baguette lengthwise. Spread the apricot mayonnaise evenly over the surface and then scatter the radicchio. First add the bacon then the turkey breast to the baguette. Fold it shut, press firmly, and slice into 4 equal-sized sections. Serve immediately, or wrap up in wax paper for your trip.

That certain something
Toast the filled baguette on a grill for about
1 minute on each side to make it even more
delicious. The turkey breast and bacon can also
be prepared on the barbecue or grill.

For 4 people
Preparation time about 20 minutes

Sandwiches with Ricotta Cheese and Figs

7oz (200g) ricotta cheese
1 tbsp olive oil
1½in (4cm) piece ginger, peeled and
   finely chopped
1 garlic clove, finely chopped or crushed
¼ tsp chili flakes
¼ tsp dried oregano
pinch of grated nutmeg
salt and freshly ground black pepper
4-5 sun-dried tomatoes (in oil), finely diced
8 slices of white bread
8 thin slices of prosciutto
3 figs, thinly sliced

1 Put the ricotta cheese into a bowl and stir in the oil. Season with the ginger, garlic, chili flakes, oregano, nutmeg, and salt and pepper. Add the sun-dried tomatoes.

2 Spread the mixture over the bread and place a slice of prosciutto on top of each one, and then lay the fig slices on the prosciutto. Place the bread slices with filled sides together and press firmly.

3 Toast the sandwiches on a grill over medium heat on both sides until golden brown. Alternatively, they can also be prepared on the stove or a camping stove. To do this, heat 2 tablespoons of olive oil in a pan, and fry the sandwiches over medium heat on both sides until golden brown. Remove from the pan, slice the filled bread in half diagonally, and serve right away—or enjoy them cold on the road.

Strawberry Sandwich

4 tbsp chocolate hazelnut spread
8 slices of white bread
3½oz (100g) strawberries, cut into
 ⅛in (3mm) thick slices
8 marshmallows, cut into ¼in (6mm)
 thick slices
3 tbsp ground almonds

1 Spread the chocolate hazelnut spread evenly over 4 slices of the bread. Place the sliced strawberries in a layer on top and cover these with the sliced marshmallows.

2 Sprinkle the almonds and top with the remaining slices of bread. Press together firmly and slice in half diagonally to serve.

Yay, there are marshmallows left over!
Spear the marshmallows on a stick and hold them over the campfire until they are browned. Or, if you don't have a fire, slide leftover marshmallows onto wooden skewers (soaked in water for at least 30 minutes beforehand), and lay these on aluminum foil on the barbecue. Wait a moment to let them cool down—then enjoy!

For 4 people · preparation time about 20 minutes

Italian-Style Sandwiches with Tahini and Tomato

2 tbsp olive oil
3 beefsteak tomatoes, cut into ½in
   (1cm) thick slices
salt and freshly ground black pepper
8 slices of white bread, crusts removed
1 garlic clove, halved
4 tbsp tahini (sesame seed paste)
2 tsp lemon juice
2 sprigs of mint leaves
pinch of dried oregano

1 Heat the oil in a pan. Sauté the tomato slices over medium heat and season with salt and pepper. In the meantime, toast the bread until crisp in a toaster or under the grill. Rub the garlic halves over the surface of the toasted slices of bread.

2 Stir the tahini into the lemon juice and season to taste with a bit of salt and pepper. Spread evenly over 4 slices of the bread and arrange the sliced tomato on top. Sprinkle the mint leaves over the tomatoes. Season with the oregano and top with the remaining 4 slices of bread. Slice diagonally and serve.

Italian-Style Sandwiches with Ricotta and Prosciutto

4 tbsp ricotta
8 slices of white bread, crusts removed
3½oz (100g) prosciutto
2 tomatoes, cut into ⅛in (3mm) thick slices
1 tbsp balsamic vinegar
1 tbsp olive oil
salt and freshly ground black pepper
handful of arugula

1 Spread the slices of bread evenly with ricotta and top 4 of the slices with the prosciutto.

2 Lay the tomatoes over the ham. Drizzle over a few drops of vinegar and oil and season generously with salt and pepper. Add the arugula over the tomatoes.

3 Place the 4 slices of bread with just ricotta cheese-side down on top of the tomato layer, pressing down firmly. Slice the sandwiches diagonally and serve.

For 4 people
Preparation time about 25 minutes

Ham and Cheddar Wraps with Honey-Mustard Sauce

2 tbsp full-fat yogurt
1 tbsp medium–hot mustard
2 tbsp honey
salt and freshly ground black pepper
8 slices of bacon
1 small romaine lettuce, halved lengthwise
   and cut into thin strips
handful of arugula
2 tomatoes
4 large wheat tortillas
4 slices Cheddar cheese
4 slices ham

1 To make the honey and mustard sauce, combine the yogurt, mustard, and honey in a bowl and season to taste with salt and pepper. Heat a pan without any oil. Place the bacon in the pan and fry over medium heat until crisp. Remove and leave to drain on paper towels.

2 Mix the lettuce with the arugula, wash, and leave to drain. Cut each tomato into 6 slices. Heat the tortillas one after another in a dry pan or on the grill over medium heat for 15 seconds each side.

3 Place a bit of lettuce and 3 slices of tomato in the center of each tortilla and drizzle over 2 tablespoons of the sauce. Place 1 slice each of Cheddar cheese and ham on the tomatoes and top with 2 slices of bacon. Fold the short side of each tortilla over the filling, fold in the long side, and roll up the tortilla as tightly as possible before serving.

Extra tasty
The assembled wraps taste particularly good toasted until crispy. Either do this under the broiler or heat them in a pan with a bit of butter. Absolutely delicious!

For 2 people
Preparation time about 15 minutes

Eggless Pancakes

1¼ cups flour
1 tsp baking powder
3 tbsp sugar
½ tsp salt
1 cup milk
2–3 drops pure vanilla extract
5 tbsp canola oil

Also
jam or chocolate hazelnut spread
(as desired)

1 Combine the flour, baking powder, sugar, and salt in a bowl. Stir in the milk (or alternatively use water or almond milk) and vanilla extract to create a smooth mixture.

2 Heat the oil in a pan. For each pancake, put 1 tablespoon of the mixture into the pan and cook over medium heat for about 1 minute on each side. Serve with jam or chocolate hazelnut spread.

Breakfast from a tube
Our pancake mixture is perfect for preparing ahead if you are able to chill it. Pour into squeeze bottles, store in the fridge, and squirt portions directly into the pan. It's super easy and will satisfy hungry campers in the morning in no time.

Keep it local

Imagine it's early in the morning and you're setting off for a market. The sun is shining, and there's plenty of hustle and bustle. Colorful stalls stand next to one another. At one stall, you spot fragrant, sun-ripened tomatoes. Mmmm... you must grab some of those!

Whether it's garden vegetables, fresh sausage, creamery cheese, or locally made wine–regional shopping is an unforgettable experience. It's a pleasure for the senses and perfect for picking up fresh produce to add to your core supplies. Bear in mind, though, that some items need to be handled carefully and kept chilled throughout your trip.

Before you set off

There are a few basic supplies that are essential for a mobile pantry, such as spices, onions, garlic, oil, flour, and coffee (see packing list, p156). Also, canned items, such as tuna and beans, that don't need refrigerating and can be bought before leaving home are highly practical. Then buy regional delicacies and fresh fruit and vegetables once you've reached your vacation destination.

Nice and cool

Dairy products (unless unopened UHT milk or almond milk), fish, and meat, which keep only for a short time, need to be stored at temperatures between 36°F and 43°F (2°C and 6°C). Keep these well chilled in airtight containers to protect them. You can judge whether something is still okay from its smell and appearance. Test before you eat: fresh foods have a neutral smell; and meat and fish should be firm, resistant to pressure, and have a good color. Since large quantities of food are difficult to accommodate in a tiny camping kitchen, it's best to shop frequently and use up fresh food as quickly as possible.

Good to know: shelf life

Fresh fish: 1 day

Beef: 3 days

Veal and pork: 2 days

Poultry: 1–2 days

Ground meat: consume on day of purchase

From the cold store

A cooler with freezer blocks will suffice for keeping drinks cold, but the more often the box is opened, the faster the contents will warm. For ingredients such as sausages, cheese, meat, fish, or opened sauces, you will need a more effective, long-term solution. Electric coolers are available in various sizes and offer different operating modes.

When purchasing a cooler, consider how noisy the box is, whether it is suitable for longer trips, and how reliably it will work at high external temperatures. Also find out the following: can the box be operated using a car battery (12 V), via the power supply system at the campsite (120 V), or with an energy-efficient solar system on the roof? If you want to keep all your options open, you will need to purchase a hybrid cooler that can also run off gas, or you could just purchase a convenient camping fridge with a mini freezer compartment.

Stack them up

Stacking items is the best way to pack a cooler, ensuring that everything stays cool and dry.

1st layer (right at the bottom):
ideally lay a grill on the bottom so that nothing sits in water from condensation.

2nd layer:
keep frozen water bottles or freezer packs here, with food in rectangular storage containers packed in between.

3rd layer:
ideally place cheese, sausages, and grilled meat on another grill and then place additional cooling elements above this.

Ideally, eggs should be chilled (see also tip on p75).

49

For 4 people
Preparation time about 30 minutes

Orange and Avocado Salad with Dijon Dressing

For the dressing

11 garlic cloves, finely chopped or crushed
2 tbsp mayonnaise
1 tbsp whole-grain Dijon mustard
2 tbsp honey
3 tbsp white wine vinegar
3 tbsp olive oil
1 tsp dried tarragon
salt and freshly ground black pepper

For the salad

5 oranges
1 pink grapefruit
1 blood orange
1 small fennel bulb, stalk removed then
    sliced into very thin strips or shredded
2 red onions, cut into thin strips
2 avocados, pitted and flesh diced
½ bunch of mint leaves

1 To make the dressing, add the garlic to the rest of the dressing
ingredients in a bowl and combine with a balloon whisk until
smooth. Season to taste with salt and pepper and set aside.

2 Cut off the peel and white pith of the oranges, grapefruit, and
blood orange. Cut the fruit into roughly ¼in (6mm) thick slices
and divide between the plates. Sprinle the fennel over the citrus fruit.

3 Lay the onions over the salad. Add the avocados, and drizzle
dressing evenly over everything. Garnish the salad with the mint
leaves and serve.

Broccoli Salad with Cashews and Roquefort Dressing

For the dressing
1¾oz (50g) Roquefort cheese (or another
   blue cheese)
1 garlic clove, finely chopped or crushed
3 tbsp white wine vinegar
1 tbsp lemon juice
1 tbsp sugar
pinch of cayenne pepper
4 tbsp olive oil
2 tbsp whole milk yogurt

For the salad
2¼lb (1kg) broccoli, cut into small florets
2 sprigs of mint, stalks removed and leaves
   roughly chopped
1 red onion, thinly sliced
½ cup blueberries
2 tbsp sunflower seeds
4 tbsp cashews
salt and freshly ground black pepper

1 To make the dressing, finely crumble the Roquefort cheese and add to a bowl with the garlic, vinegar, lemon juice, and sugar. Crush the Roquefort cheese with a fork until it has almost completely dissolved. Put the remaining dressing ingredients into a large salad bowl and whisk until well combined using a balloon whisk. Then add the Roquefort mixture and combine.

2 Combine the broccoli, mint, onion, blueberries, sunflower seeds, and cashews. Drizzle over the dressing and mix everything carefully. Let stand for about 1 hour, and then season to taste with salt and pepper before serving.

Eat it all!
Often broccoli stalks end up, needlessly, in the trash, even though they are perfect for making soup. Peel and finely chop 1lb 2oz (500g) of broccoli stalk. Add to a pan with 1 cup peeled and quartered potatoes and 3 cups vegetable stock. Simmer for 25 minutes and purée with a handheld blender. Add ½ cup cream and season with nutmeg and salt and pepper.

Green Asparagus Salad with Feta Cheese

For the salad

14oz (400g) can kidney beans
1lb 5oz (600g) green asparagus
1 cup green beans
2 carrots, peeled and grated
1 cup feta cheese, cut into
 ½in (1cm) cubes
bread rolls or flatbread, to serve

For the dressing

3 tbsp sherry vinegar
1 tbsp sugar
1 tsp dried oregano
1 tsp medium-hot mustard
4 tbsp olive oil
salt and freshly ground black pepper

1 Pour the kidney beans into a colander, rinse, and leave to drain. Break off the woody end of the asparagus spears and peel the lower 1½in (4cm) of each spear. Slice diagonally into 1¾–2in (4–5cm) long pieces. Slice the green beans diagonally into roughly 1½in (4cm) long pieces.

2 Bring 4 cups salted water to a boil in a pan, and cook the asparagus and green beans for 6 minutes, until just tender. Drain, plunge into cold water, and leave to drain in a colander.

3 Combine the grated carrot, diced cheese, kidney beans, asparagus, and green beans in a salad bowl.

4 Stir the dressing ingredients together in a bowl and season to taste with salt and pepper. Drizzle over the salad and arrange on 4 plates, and then serve with fresh bread rolls or flatbread.

Tomato and Corn Salad with Chickpeas

10oz (285g) can corn
14oz (400g) can chickpeas
1 garlic clove, finely chopped
   or crushed
3 tbsp mascarpone
3 tbsp white balsamic vinegar
2 tbsp honey
1 tbsp mayonnaise
½ bunch of basil, stalks removed and
   leaves chopped
salt and freshly ground black pepper
8 tomatoes, seeded and quartered
8 radishes, halved
1 red onion, very finely sliced
3 scallions

1 Strain the corn and chickpeas, rinse, and then leave to drain. Add the garlic to a salad bowl with the mascarpone, vinegar, honey, and mayonnaise, and stir until you have a smooth sauce. Add the chopped basil leaves to the salad dressing and season to taste with salt and pepper.

2 Chop the tomato quarters into ¼in (6mm) thick strips. Slice the radish halves into ⅛in (3mm) thick slices. Slice the scallions into ¼in (6mm) wide rings. Add the onion, radishes, scallions, corn, and chickpeas to the salad dressing, fold everything gently together, divide between 4 plates, and serve.

For 4 people
Preparation time about 25 minutes

Strawberry Salad with Mozzarella

For the salad

2 tbsp butter
3½oz (100g) mie noodles, cut into
 ¾in (2cm) pieces
4 tbsp chopped almonds
3 tbsp sunflower seeds
2 handfuls of baby spinach, large leaves
 chopped
1 romaine lettuce, stalk removed, quartered,
 then cut in ¼in (6mm) pieces
1 cup strawberries, cut in ¼in
 (6mm) pieces
3½oz (100g) Parmesan cheese shavings
7oz (200g) mini mozzarella balls

For the dressing

1 garlic clove, finely chopped or pressed
4 tbsp sugar
6 tbsp red wine vinegar
4 tbsp canola oil
1 tsp paprika
salt and freshly ground black pepper

1 Melt the butter in a large pan and fry the noodles, almonds, and sunflower seeds over medium heat until golden brown. Remove from the stove and let cool.

2 Combine the spinach, lettuce, strawberries, Parmesan cheese, and mozzarella in a salad bowl and set aside.

3 To make the dressing, mix the garlic, sugar, and vinegar together in a bowl until the sugar has dissolved. Stir in the oil and paprika and season to taste with salt and pepper. Mix the salad with the dressing and divide between 4 plates. Sprinkle with the crunchy noodle mixture and serve.

Keep leaves fresh
No room for a salad spinner in your luggage? No problem. Wrap salad leaves in a resealable freezer bag or a damp kitchen towel before chilling, and they will stay fresh for 2 to 3 days.

For 4 people
Preparation time about 25 minutes

Couscous Salad with Grapefruit Dressing

1 cup vegetable stock
1⅓ cups couscous
2 pink grapefruit, juice reserved
½ bunch of basil leaves, finely chopped
3 sprigs of mint leaves, finely chopped
2 tsp whole-grain Dijon mustard
1 tbsp honey
2 tbsp white wine vinegar
3 tbsp olive oil
salt and freshly ground black pepper
1 leek, quartered lengthwise, then cut into
   ¼in (6mm) wide pieces
½ cup cherry tomatoes, halved

1 Bring the stock to a boil in a pan. Stir in the couscous, remove the pan from the heat, and let the grains swell for 5 minutes. Fluff with a fork to separate the grains and let stand for a further 5 minutes.

2 Cut the peel off the grapefruit with a knife, making sure the white pith is also removed. Cut segments of fruit between the membranes, working over a bowl while doing this to catch any juice. Once you have segmented the grapefruit, squeeze out any remaining juice and slice each grapefruit segment into 3 pieces.

3 Add the basil and mint to the grapefruit juice along with the mustard, honey, vinegar, and oil. Stir everything together to make the dressing and season to taste with salt and pepper.

4 Combine the couscous, leek, grapefruit, and cherry tomatoes in a bowl and drizzle with the dressing. Divide the salad between 4 plates and serve.

Keep it simple
There are several types of camping utensils: you can get folding designs, a complete set that fits into a practical bag, utensils with carabiner hooks for easy attaching, or–for the minimalists–the "spork." A spork is a single utensil with a fork on one side and a spoon on the other!

For 4 people
Preparation time about 40 minutes

Grilled Radicchio Salad

For the dressing
4 tbsp olive oil
2 tbsp sherry vinegar
2 tsp medium–hot mustard
1 tbsp honey
salt and freshly ground black pepper

For the salad
6 shallots, stems removed, quartered
2 tbsp olive oil
1 radicchio, halved, stalks removed, then
   sliced into ½in (1cm) thick strips
1 small red lollo rosso (red leaf) lettuce,
   torn into bite-sized pieces

1 Put the dressing ingredients into a small bowl and stir. Season to taste with salt and set aside.

2 Brush the shallots with 1 tablespoon of the olive oil, season with salt and pepper, and cook over a hot barbecue grill for 5 minutes. Move to a cooler part of the grill and continue to grill over low heat for 12 minutes, until the shallots are soft. Close the lid (if you have one) on the barbecue during this process. Remove the shallots from the grill and set aside.

3 Brush the radicchio with the remaining olive oil and season with salt and pepper. Place the pieces cut-side down and cook for 2–3 minutes over low heat with the barbecue lid closed if possible, until the edges begin to go brown and crisp. Remove from the grill and let cool slightly.

4 Divide the lollo rosso between 4 plates. Sprinkle the shallots over the lettuce, and divide the radicchio evenly between the plates. Drizzle everything with the dressing and serve.

For 4 people
Preparation time about 40 minutes · infusion time 20 minutes

Country Potato Salad

3lb 3oz (1.5kg) waxy new potatoes, peeled
 if preferred
4 tbsp canola oil
1 red pepper, seeded and cut into
 1½in (3 x 4cm) pieces
2 red onions, finely sliced
3 tbsp red wine vinegar
4 tbsp mustard
1 tbsp sugar
salt and freshly ground black pepper
½ bunch of flat-leaf parsley, leaves and
 stems roughly chopped

1 Boil the potatoes in salted water for 25 minutes, drain, and let cool slightly before cutting into 8 pieces or slicing into approximately ½in (1cm) thick discs.

2 Heat the oil in a large pan on the gas stove or barbecue. Sauté the pepper and onions, stirring constantly, over medium heat for 2 minutes. Add the potatoes to the pan and continue to fry for another 6 minutes.

3 Combine the vinegar, mustard, and sugar in a large bowl. Add the potatoes and vegetables and mix carefully. Season to taste with salt and pepper and let stand for 20 minutes.

4 Add the parsley to the potato salad and fold it in. Adjust the salad seasoning with additional salt and pepper, if required, and serve.

Apple and Spinach Salad with Cranberry Dressing

For the dressing

2 tbsp orange marmalade
3 tbsp white wine vinegar
1 tsp medium–hot mustard
salt and freshly ground black pepper
4 tbsp canola oil
3 tbsp dried cranberries

For the salad

5 handfuls of baby spinach, stalks removed
   and leaves torn
1 small head of radicchio, stalk removed,
   quartered, and sliced diagonally into
   ¼in (6mm) strips
1 red onion, cut into wafer-thin strips
2 apples, such as Granny Smith, core
   removed, cut into ⅛in (3mm) slices
3 tbsp pecans or pumpkin seeds,
   roughly chopped

1 Stir together the marmalade, vinegar, mustard, 1 teaspoon of salt, and 2 pinches of pepper in a salad bowl until the salt has dissolved. Add the oil and cranberries and stir.

2 Add the spinach, radicchio, onion, and apples to the salad bowl, and combine with the dressing. Season the salad to taste with additional salt and pepper, if required, and divide between 4 plates. Sprinkle with the chopped nuts or seeds and serve.

Voyage of discovery

Shopping away from home is much more fun than at your usual supermarket. You can take your time picking up your provisions and admire all the regional specialties and different products. Dive in! Also, ask at the campsite about weekly regional markets, where delicious local produce will await you.

Cooking outdoors-a great experience!

Creating meals in an improvised, open-air kitchen offers an enormous amount of freedom. Even dealing with the stove is part of the whole camping experience—it's a real outdoor adventure!

There are many types of camping stoves available, so it can be difficult deciding which one is best for your needs. Every camper has her own preconceptions and will gladly talk shop on the subject. The crucial thing when choosing your equipment is to work out what your requirements are.

Safe, clean, and simple gas stoves

Various types of fuel can be used for heating up your food. A popular camping option is a gas stove. These come in a number of different sizes, with one or two burners, and can be run using butane, propane, or some combination of these fuels. They are super easy to use! You can get pierceable gas canisters, or valve canisters with screw or clip-fit connectors. Gas stoves aren't heavy; on average, they weigh 2½oz (70g). The canisters are a bit heavier, and you should ideally have a spare one as a backup. Energy-saving solutions are particularly popular for campers, because the lower the fuel consumption, the fewer supplies you need to pack. As long as you have an adequate supply of gas, you will be ensured a reliable mode of cooking and high performance that will bring 4 cups of water to a boil in about 5 minutes.

Reliable gas stoves

It takes extreme cold to impact the performance of gasoline stoves, which perform very well even in icy temperatures. Another advantage is that gasoline can be bought everywhere. However, these camping stoves are not quite as convenient to use as gas stoves; they emit a stronger smell and always have to be cleaned thoroughly. One possible solution for an around-the-world trip or an expedition is the multi-fuel stove, which is designed to run on either gasoline or butane or propane.

Other options

Another fairly reliable option is the spirit stove. The downside of these is that they aren't as easy to control, they have only a moderate heat output, and they can cause a buildup of soot on your pans. Solid fuel stoves, which run on hexamine fuel tablets, are small and lightweight. They are suitable for simple meals that just need warming up. Electric stoves always require a power connection at the campsite. They are very simple to operate and function exactly like a normal stove but are very restricting.

Five practical camping stove tips

1. Read the operating instructions and practice before you set off.
2. Acquire a windbreak.
3. Use the equipment outside (unless specifically suited for indoor use).
4. Make sure the stove is secure when you set it up.
5. Don't forget the saucepan lid—it will save energy.

Decision-making guide when purchasing

Ask yourself the following questions and seek advice accordingly:

Where am I traveling to? Not all places sell suitable gas canisters.

How am I getting from A to B? Flammable substances such as gasoline, propane, or alcohol are prohibited in aircraft.

Where will I be cooking once there? Different conditions will apply on a trek through the mountains than at a family-friendly campground area.

How much does my luggage weigh? Choose the number and weight of your stoves and canisters accordingly.

Fettuccine Alfredo

1 onion
2 carrots, peeled
1 leek, sliced lengthwise
3 celery stalks
7oz (200g) ham
2 tbsp butter
2 cups cream
2 tsp cornstarch
1lb 2oz (500g) fettuccine
½ bunch of flat-leaf parsley, stalks removed
    and leaves roughly chopped
3½oz (100g) Parmesan cheese, finely grated
salt and freshly ground black pepper

1 Chop all the vegetables and the ham into ¼in (6mm) cubes.

2 Melt the butter in a pan over medium heat. Add the vegetables and diced ham and sauté for 3 minutes, stirring constantly. Add the cream then stir the cornstarch into ½ cup water and add this, too. Simmer over low heat, stirring occasionally, for 15 minutes.

3 While the sauce is cooking, bring 3½ pints (2 liters) of salted water to a boil in a second pan. Cook the fettuccine according to the package instructions until al dente.

4 Add the parsley to the sauce at the end of the cooking time along with the Parmesan cheese. Stir and season to taste with salt and pepper.

5 Drain the fettuccine and divide between 4 plates. Serve the pasta with the sauce.

One-pot cuisine
If you would like to make the pasta in a single pan, just proceed as described above, but before the simmering stage in Step 2, add the pasta to the pan. Pour over enough vegetable stock to cover all the ingredients, and then cook everything over moderate heat, stirring occasionally. If too much liquid boils off, just add a bit more water.

Pasta Bolognese alla Nonna

2 tbsp olive oil
9oz (250g) ground beef
1 onion, finely diced
1 garlic clove, finely chopped or crushed
14oz (400g) tomato purée
3 tbsp sugar
2 tsp chili flakes
salt
14oz (400g) spaghetti
½ bunch of basil, stalks removed and
   leaves chopped
3½oz (100g) hard cheese, such as
   Parmesan, Pecorino Romano, or
   Gruyère, coarsley grated

1 Heat the oil in a pan. Cook the ground beef over high heat for about 5 minutes until browned. Add the onion and garlic and continue to cook for another 2 minutes.

2 Add the tomato purée to the pan along with the sugar and chili flakes and stir gently. Cover the pan with a lid and simmer over low heat for 15 minutes, stirring occasionally.

3 While the sauce is cooking, bring 3½ pints (2 liters) of salted water to a boil in a second pan. Cook the spaghetti according to the package instructions until al dente.

4 Add the basil to the sauce and season to taste with salt.

5 Drain the spaghetti in a colander and divide between 4 plates. Serve with the sauce and the cheese sprinkled on top.

A meandering road trip
If you need to get somewhere fast, the freeway is usually the quickest route. But if you want to make the most of your vacation destination, we suggest taking alternative routes now and then. Some country roads have breathtaking views that can make the trip as enjoyable as the destination.

Goulash with Paprika and Potatoes

2 tbsp canola oil
1lb 2oz (500g) mixed strips of beef and pork
salt and freshly ground black pepper
3 onions, diced
2 garlic cloves, finely chopped or crushed
2 tbsp all-purpose flour
2 tbsp tomato purée
1½ cups cold water
1 tbsp beef (or other meat) stock, or 1 beef
  stock cube
1 tsp caraway
2 tsp paprika
2 red peppers, seeded and cut into
  1½in (4cm) cubes
8 waxy potatoes, peeled and quartered
4 tbsp sour cream

1 Heat the oil in a pan. Season the meat with salt and pepper and sauté over high heat for 8 minutes, until browned. Add the diced onion and continue to fry over medium heat for a further 5 minutes. Stir in the garlic and flour and sweat for 1 minute, and then stir in the tomato purée and cook for 3 minutes.

2 Pour in the cold water, add the stock, caraway, and paprika, cover, and leave to stew over low heat for 40 minutes. Then add the peppers to the pan and stew for another 20 minutes.

3 Add the potatoes to a second pan. Cover with water, season with 1 teaspoon of salt, bring to a boil, and cook for 20 minutes, and then drain.

4 Season the goulash to taste with salt and pepper and divide between 4 plates. Garnish each portion with 1 tablespoon of sour cream and serve with the potatoes.

For 2 people · preparation time about 35 minutes

Pan-Fried Sausage and Leek with Potatoes

1 tbsp butter
14oz (400g) waxy potatoes, peeled
  and cut into ¼in (6mm) strips
2–4 smoked sausages (about 5½oz/
  150g), cut into ½in (1cm) slices
1 leek, halved lengthwise then sliced
  diagonally into thin strips
2 red onions, sliced into thin strips
1 large beefsteak tomato, cut into ¾in
  (2cm) cubes
4 tbsp soft cheese with herbs
salt and freshly ground black pepper

1 Heat the butter in a large pan. Sauté the potatoes and sausages over medium heat for 5 minutes, stirring constantly. Add the leek and onions and continue to fry for a further 3 minutes. Add the diced tomatoes to the pan, stir, and cook everything for an additional 10 minutes over medium heat, stirring occasionally.

2 Stir in the soft cheese until it has completely dissolved. Season to taste with salt and pepper, divide between 2 plates, and serve.

Croque Madame

2 tsp Dijon mustard
2 tbsp crème fraîche
8 slices white bread
4 slices ham
4 slices Gruyère cheese
4 tbsp butter
4 eggs
salt and freshly ground black pepper

1 Stir the mustard and crème fraîche together. Spread this thinly over the slices of bread. Top 4 of the slices with ham and cheese. Cover with the remaining 4 slices of bread and press down slightly. Heat some of the butter in a pan and fry the croques (sandwiches) in batches over medium heat for 2–3 minutes each side.

2 Meanwhile, heat the remaining butter in a second pan and fry the eggs. Season with salt and pepper. Divide the croques between 4 plates, top with the fried eggs, and serve.

Do eggs really need to go in the fridge?
Obviously space is at a premium in a camping kitchen, but ideally eggs should be stored in a fridge. Their natural protective layer means they will keep unrefrigerated for 18 days after they are laid, but when you're traveling, it's best to err on the safe side and get them chilled right away. Once eggs have been refrigerated, they will stay fresh for longer.

For 2 people
Preparation time about 20 minutes

Three Omelet Options

Spanish Omelet

6 eggs
salt and freshly ground black pepper
3½oz (100g) chorizo, cut into
 small cubes
1 red pepper, seeded and cut into
 small cubes
1 waxy potato, cut into small cubes
2 tbsp butter

1 Crack 3 of the eggs into a bowl, season with salt and pepper, and whisk gently with a fork then set aside. In a separate bowl, combine the chorizo, pepper, and potato.

2 Heat 1 tablespoon of the butter in a pan (9½in/24cm diameter) over moderate heat until it foams. Add half the chorizo mixture and fry for 6 minutes, stirring occasionally. Add the beaten eggs and tilt the pan to distribute evenly. Cover and cook the omelet for about 3 minutes. Carefully fold it over using a spatula and continue to cook, covered, for a further 3 minutes.

3 Slide the omelet onto a plate, and wrap the plate in a clean kitchen towel to keep it warm. Make a second omelet, as above, from the remaining chorizo mixture and eggs.

Austrian Omelet

3½oz (100g) bacon, cut into strips
6 eggs
salt and freshly ground black pepper
3½oz (100g) hard cheese, such
 as Emmental or Parmesan,
 coarsely grated

1 Add half the bacon to a dry pan (9½in/24cm diameter), and cook over medium heat until crisp all over.

2 Crack 3 of the eggs into a bowl, season with salt and pepper, and whisk gently with a fork. Add the eggs and half the cheese to the pan and tilt to distribute evenly. Cover the pan and cook the omelet for 3 minutes. Carefully fold it over using a spatula and continue to cook, covered, for a further 3 minutes.

3 Slide the omelet onto a plate, and wrap the plate in a clean kitchen towel to keep it warm. Make a second omelet from the remaining ingredients, as above.

Swedish Omelet

7oz (200g) cooked shrimp
1 garlic clove, finely chopped
  or crushed
2 tbsp olive oil
6 eggs
salt and freshly ground black pepper
½ bunch of dill, finely chopped

1 Place the shrimp in a colander, rinse, and leave to drain. Stir the garlic into the olive oil. Crack 3 of the eggs into a bowl, season with salt and pepper, and whisk gently with a fork.

2 Heat 1 tablespoon of the garlic oil in a pan (9½in/24cm diameter), and sauté half the shrimp over moderate heat on all sides. Add the beaten eggs and tilt the pan to distribute evenly. Cover the pan and cook the omelet for 3 minutes. Carefully fold it over using a spatula and continue to cook, covered, for a further 3 minutes.

3 Slide the omelet onto a plate, and wrap the plate in a clean kitchen towel to keep it warm. Make a second omelet using the remaining shrimp and egg mixture, as above. Sprinkle the cooked omelets with the dill and serve immediately.

Cheese and Vegetable Gnocchi

2 cups all-purpose flour
1 cup Gouda cheese, roughly grated
1 tsp ground turmeric
salt and freshly ground black pepper
3½oz (100g) sugar snap peas, halved
   lengthwise then cut into ¼in (6mm)
   wide strips
1 carrot, peeled and coarsely grated
2 tbsp vegetable stock

1 Stir the flour into 1 cup water in a bowl. Add the Gouda cheese, turmeric, 1 tsp salt, 2 pinches of pepper, sugar snap peas, and carrots, and work with your hands to combine. Let stand for 15 minutes.

2 Meanwhile, in a pan, bring 2¾ pints water to a boil and dissolve the stock in it. Lower the temperature and add 2 teaspoons of the cheesy mixture. Continue with the remaining mixture, and then let steep over medium heat for about 12 minutes. Divide the gnocchi between 2 plates and serve with some of the stock.

Frying pan option
You can also use this mixture to make vegetable and cheese flatbreads in a frying pan. To do this, heat some oil, add about 1 tbsp of the mixture to the pan for each flatbread, and fry for 4 minutes on each side over moderate heat.

For 2 people
Preparation time about 25 minutes

Greek Pan-Cooked Pasta

3¼ cups orzo (rice-shaped pasta pieces)
3 tbsp olive oil
1 eggplant, cut into about ¾in (2cm) cubes
1 zucchini, cut into about ¾in (2cm) cubes
1 red onion, finely diced
1 garlic clove, finely chopped or crushed
3 tomatoes, quartered
7oz (200g) feta cheese, cut into ¾in
  (2cm) cubes
2 tsp dried oregano
½ tsp dried thyme
salt and freshly ground black pepper

1 Cook the pasta in a pan with 2 cups salted water according to the package instructions. Pour into a colander, rinse in cold water, and leave to drain.

2 Heat the oil in a large pan. Sauté the eggplant and zucchini in the pan over high heat for 3 minutes, stirring constantly. Lower the temperature to medium heat. Add the onion and garlic to the vegetables and fry for a further 3 minutes. Add the tomatoes, deglaze with 4 tablespoons of water, reduce the temperature to low heat, and continue cooking for a further 10 minutes.

3 Add the pasta, feta, oregano, and thyme to the vegetables in the pan and heat for 2 minutes. If needed, add 1–2 tablespoons of water to prevent the pasta from sticking. Season to taste with salt and pepper and serve.

Vegetable favorites for when you're on the move
There's always a chronic shortage of space in coolers. So when choosing vegetables for a trip, we opt for ones that don't really need to be kept chilled—such as tomatoes, zucchini, or eggplants. This frees up space in our cooler for items that spoil easily, such as fish, meat, and dairy products.

For 4 people
Preparation time about 30 minutes

Vegetable Stew with Gnocchi

3½oz (100g) bacon, cut into ¼in (6mm) wide strips
4 carrots, chopped into ½in (1cm) cubes
2 kohlrabi, chopped into ½in (1cm) cubes
2 onions, finely diced
3 celery stalks, cut into ½in (1cm) pieces
5½ cups water
3 tbsp vegetable stock
14oz (400g) potato gnocchi
½ bunch of flat-leaf parsley, leaves roughly chopped
salt and freshly ground black pepper

1 Heat a pan without any oil or fat. Fry the bacon over medium heat for 3 minutes, stirring constantly. Add the carrots, kohlrabi, onion, and celery, and sweat for 3 minutes in the fat that has been released from the bacon.

2 Pour in the water, stir in the stock, and bring to a boil. Simmer over low to medium heat for 20 minutes, stirring occasionally. After 10 minutes, add the gnocchi and continue to cook.

3 Add the parsley to the cooked stew, season everything to taste with salt and pepper, divide between 4 plates, and serve.

Into the thermos

Are you off hiking in the mountains or dashing through foothills on your bicycle? Not surprisingly, active campers get absolutely ravenous when they're out trekking or cycling. The perfect solution is a preprepared vegetable stew in a vacuum flask. Just transfer the cooked dish into a suitable thermos while it is still hot and enjoy it when you take a break—you'll be full of energy when you set off again.

Makes about 20 croquettes
Preparation time about 45 minutes

Cauliflower Cheese Croquettes

For the croquettes
1 cauliflower (about 2¼lb/1kg)
1 onion, finely diced
5½oz (150g) Comté cheese (or Gruyère),
  coarsely grated
½ bunch of flat-leaf parsley, leaves
  roughly chopped
2 eggs
1½ cups white bread crumbs, plus extra
  if needed
grated nutmeg
salt
4 cups canola oil

For the sauce
1 tbsp butter
1 tbsp all-purpose flour
1 tbsp lemon juice
1 cup milk
1 onion, finely diced
bunch of chives, finely chopped
grated nutmeg
salt

1 Split the cauliflower into small florets, wash, and cook in salted water for about 15 minutes, until soft. Drain in a colander, making sure you retain 1 cup of the cooking water. Let the cauliflower cool for 10 minutes.

2 Transfer the cauliflower to a bowl and mash it with a fork or potato masher. Add the onion, cheese, parsley, eggs, and bread crumbs, and work until combined. Season with nutmeg and salt. If necessary, add some more bread crumbs until the mixture is firm enough to shape. Use your hands to make about 20 similar-sized croquettes and set aside.

3 To make the sauce, melt the butter in a pan over medium heat, stir in the flour, and cook for 30 seconds. Pour in the lemon juice, milk, and retained cooking water. Add the chopped onion and chives, bring to a boil, stirring constantly, and then simmer for 2 minutes over low heat.

4 Meanwhile, heat the oil in a separate pan. Place the cauliflower croquettes in a deep colander, lower them into the hot oil, and fry over medium heat until golden brown. Remove and leave to drain on kitchen towels.

5 Season the sauce to taste with nutmeg and salt and serve with the croquettes.

Feel like a change?
Instead of making croquettes, you can also shape the mixture into flatbreads and fry them in hot oil in a pan over medium heat for 3–4 minutes on each side.

Pasta with Cabbage and Bacon

14oz (400g) fusilli
3½oz (100g) lard
5½oz (150g) bacon
2 onions, diced
1 head white cabbage (around 1lb 2oz/500g), stalk removed and cut into ¾in (2cm) cubes
1 tsp sugar
½ tsp caraway
1 tsp paprika
salt and freshly ground black pepper

1 Bring 3½ pints salted water to a boil in a pan for the pasta. Cook the pasta in the boiling water according to the package instructions until al dente.

2 While the pasta is cooking, melt the lard in a large pan. Fry the bacon and onions over medium heat until golden brown. Add the cabbage and cook for about 12 minutes. Sprinkle over the sugar, stir, and allow to caramelize slightly.

3 Season the vegetables with caraway and paprika then add salt and pepper to taste. Pour the pasta into a colander, leave to drain briefly, and then mix with the cabbage in the pan. Divide between 4 plates and serve.

One-pot version
If you have only one burner, the cabbage can be prepared in the same pan used for cooking the pasta. Just add the pasta again at the end, stir everything well, and enjoy.

Born to be wild

Into the wilderness!

If you're looking for somewhere to camp to get back to nature, make sure you find out exactly where you're allowed to pitch a tent. In some areas, such as developed recreation areas, primitive camping is prohibited, while other places are very relaxed about it. If you are spending the night in a state or national park, check beforehand whether there is any limit on the number of visitors each day and whether you have to make a reservation, where you are allowed to light a fire, and what arrangements there are in terms of water supplies.

What do you need for wild camping?

Whether you're traveling by car or bike or you are on foot makes a massive difference when you're wilderness camping. If you are carrying your tent, sleeping bag, and all your cooking equipment in your backpack, you will obviously be restricted and will need to carry the absolute minimum. Pack only small, lightweight items, and make sure that everything is functional and, ideally, waterproof.

Adventurous ingredients

Wilderness campers have very limited options when it comes to keeping food cool, such as a hole in the ground or a cold stream. In any case, who wants to carry huge quantities of food into the wilderness? Handy, durable snacks are ideal for an occasional energy boost (see recipes from p24). And once you've worked up a real appetite in the great outdoors, you can satisfy your hunger with one of the instant meals on p90, which need only hot water to rehydrate them. Freeze-dried onions are useful, as are other products such as powdered milk and garlic granules, which can be found in supermarkets. Freeze-dried meat and other more luxurious ingredients can be bought from specialized outdoor stores or online.

Outdoors survival

If you want to immerse yourself truly in nature, you will need to do some thorough research in advance to ensure you are well informed before you set off on your trip. Carrying water is heavy work, but "wild" water can make you sick if it isn't collected at the right location or boiled or filtered properly. Also, eat berries, mushrooms, and herbs that you've collected only if you can clearly recognize and identify them and are 100 percent sure that they are not poisonous.

Wild kitchen

Use the following tips as a guide when cooking over a campfire:

* use dry wood as fuel.
* before you start cooking, let the fire burn until the combustible material has turned white. Don't cook over flames that are still leaping up!
* use a cast-iron pan that doesn't have any plastic parts. For grilling, place a grill over the embers.
* prepare your ingredients thoroughly in advance, because cooking over a campfire is a hot business and things cook in a matter of minutes.
* use all the different areas of the fire: different recipes may be best cooked over small flames, or in the embers or the ashes.
* test to see if food is cooked: the cooking time will depend on the heat and the distance from the embers.

"Fast" Food from a Bag

If you're spending the night in the middle of nowhere, you probably won't want to carry a lot of supplies, so rustling up some freeze-dried food is really convenient. Instant dishes that you just pour water on to rehydrate used to be very popular. However, homemade versions not only taste a whole lot better, but they also offer far more variety and are pretty cool. These mini-gourmet meals are definitely comfort food from a bag!

Instant Couscous with Apricots and Macadamia Nuts

2 tbsp macadamia nuts, roughly chopped
3 tbsp dried apricots, quartered
5 tbsp couscous
2 tbsp freeze-dried diced chicken
1½ tsp chicken stock, or 1 chicken stock cube
¼ tsp dried thyme
¼ tsp garlic granules
1 tsp onion granules
2 pinches of ground black pepper

1 Toast the nuts in a dry pan until golden brown. Place all the ingredients in a freezer bag and seal.

2 When you're ready to cook, bring 1½ cups water to a boil in a pan then remove from heat. Add the contents of the freezer bag, stir, and let stand for 6–8 minutes, stirring occasionally.

Instant Curry Rice with Cashews

3 tbsp cashews
1 cup parboiled basmati rice
2 tbsp freeze-dried diced chicken
3 tbsp freeze-dried mixed vegetables
1½ tsp chicken stock, or 1 chicken stock cube
1½ tsp curry powder
1 tsp onion granules
¼ tsp garlic granules
2 pinches of ground black pepper

1 Toast the cashews in a dry pan until golden brown. Add all the ingredients to a freezer bag and seal.

2 When you're ready to cook, bring 1½ cups water to a boil in a pan. Stir in the contents of the freezer bag, remove from heat, and cover with a lid. Let stand for 9 minutes, stirring everything well after 3–4 minutes.

Creamy Instant Noodles
with Mushrooms and Pine Nuts

2 tbsp pine nuts
2 handfuls vermicelli (about 2³⁄₄oz/80g)
2 tbsp freeze-dried diced chicken
2 tbsp dried mushrooms
1½ tsp chicken stock, or 1 chicken stock cube
3 tbsp grated Parmesan
2 tbsp powdered milk
2 tsp cornstarch
2 tsp herbes de Provence
¼ tsp garlic granules
2 pinches of ground black pepper

1 Toast the pine nuts in a dry pan until golden brown. Add all the ingredients to a freezer bag and seal.

2 When you're ready to cook, put the contents of the freezer bag into a pan with 1⅓ cups water. Bring to a boil while stirring, and then remove from heat and cover with a lid. Let stand for 9 minutes, stirring everything well after 3–4 minutes.

Mexican Instant Rice
with Chicken

1 cup parboiled basmati rice
2 tbsp freeze-dried diced chicken
3 tbsp freeze-dried corn
2 tbsp freeze-dried tomatoes
1½ tsp chicken stock, or 1 chicken stock cube
1½ tsp chili flakes
¼ tsp ground cumin
¼ tsp dried oregano
½ tsp ground coriander
1 tsp onion granules
¼ tsp garlic granules
2 pinches of ground black pepper

1 Add all the ingredients to a freezer bag and seal.

2 When you're ready to cook, bring 1½ cups water to a boil in a pan then remove from heat. Stir in the contents of the freezer bag and let stand for 6–8 minutes, stirring occasionally.

Chicken and Vegetable Mix with Sautéed Potatoes

12oz (340g) can corn
6 tbsp canola oil, divided use
8 waxy potatoes, cut into ¼in (6mm)
  thick slices
1lb 2oz (500g) chicken breast fillet, cut into
  1½in (4cm) cubes
3 carrots, peeled and chopped into ¾in
  (2cm) cubes
2 red peppers, deseeded and cut diagonally
  into ½in (1cm) thick strips
2 celery stalks, cut diagonally into ½in (1cm)
  thick strips
1 red chile, seeded and finely chopped
2 tbsp honey
2 tbsp soy sauce
½ cup water
1 onion, diced
salt and freshly ground black pepper

1 Pour the corn into a colander, rinse, and leave to drain. Heat 4 tablespoons of the oil in a pan. Sauté the sliced potatoes over medium heat for 25 minutes, turning occasionally but not too often so the potatoes turn nice and crisp.

2 After about 10 minutes, heat the remaining oil in a pan. Fry the chicken breast over high heat for 1 minute on both sides. Add the carrots, peppers, and celery, and continue to fry for 3 minutes, stirring constantly. Add the chile, honey, and soy sauce to the chicken pan, stir, and then pour in the water. Cover with a lid and cook over low heat for 10 minutes. Remove the lid and simmer over high heat until the liquid has almost entirely evaporated. Season to taste with salt and pepper.

3 About 5 minutes before the end of the potato cooking time, add the onion to the potatoes and continue to cook. Season the potatoes to taste with salt and pepper. Arrange with the chicken and vegetable mix on 4 plates and serve.

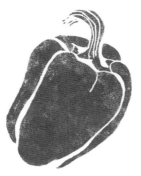

Sweet Potato and Pepper Stew

14oz (400g) can butter beans
2 tbsp butter
1 garlic clove, finely chopped or crushed
1 large sweet potato (about 12oz/350g),
  peeled and cut into ¾in (2cm) cubes
1 red pepper, seeded and cut into
  ½in (1cm) wide strips
1 yellow pepper, seeded and cut into
  ½in (1cm) wide strips
2 celery stalks, cut into ¾in (2cm)
  wide pieces
2 tomatoes, quartered
½ cup water
3 sprigs of sage leaves, sliced into thin
  strips, or 2 tsp dried sage
salt and freshly ground black pepper

1 Pour the beans into a colander, rinse, and leave to drain.

2 Heat the butter in a pan. Sweat the garlic over medium heat for 1 minute. Add the sweet potato cubes, peppers, and celery, and sauté for 3 minutes, stirring constantly. Add the tomatoes and beans then pour in the water and stir. Cover the pan with a lid and simmer over low heat for 12 minutes.

3 Add the sage to the vegetables then season the stew with salt and pepper. Divide between 2 plates and serve.

Rattling in the box
To prevent camping glasses and cups from constantly clattering while you are driving, use plate, cup, and glass holders, available from specialized stores. If you don't have kitchen storage while camping, use a large, sealable plastic box to store your utensils. These kinds of storage containers can be stacked up creatively in your mobile home.

For 2 people
Preparation time about 30 minutes

Spicy Meat Risotto

3½ tbsp Parmesan cheese, finely grated
1 tbsp canola oil
9oz (250g) ground meat, your choice of
    beef, pork, veal, or turkey
1 onion, finely diced
2 garlic cloves, finely chopped or pressed
2 red chiles, seeded and finely chopped
2 cups risotto rice
3 cups warm water
1 tbsp vegetable stock
salt and freshly ground black pepper
2 tbsp sour cream, to garnish

1 Put the Parmesan in a bowl and set aside. Heat the oil in a pan. Sauté the ground meat over high heat until it begins to brown. Add the onion, garlic, and chile and fry for 2 minutes. Stir in the rice followed by the warm water.

2 Stir in the stock, reduce the temperature, and simmer over low heat for 20 minutes, stirring occasionally. If the liquid cooks off before the rice has cooked, add some more water a tablespoon at a time. Ideally, all the liquid should have been absorbed by the rice at the end of the cooking time.

3 Take the pan off the heat and fold the Parmesan into the risotto. Season to taste with salt and pepper and divide the risotto between 2 plates. Garnish each portion with 1 tablespoon of sour cream and serve.

Ground meat is the best!

Ground meat is a real diva when compared with other meat. This sensitive soul should be bought fresh on the day you intend to cook it. If you buy shrink-wrapped ground meat, make sure you observe the expiration date on the package. And always keep it chilled!

Paella

10oz (300g) mussels
8 chicken drumsticks
salt and freshly ground black pepper
2 tbsp olive oil
1 red onion, cut into fine strips
2 garlic cloves, finely chopped
  or crushed
1½ cups risotto rice
1 cup dry white wine
1 tbsp chicken stock, or 1 chicken
  stock cube
about 1g saffron
2 cups hot water
2 bay leaves
1 red pepper, seeded and cut into
  fine strips
12 shrimp, peeled and deveined
7oz (200g) peas, shelled
1 lemon, cut into quarters, to serve

1 Discard any damaged or open mussels that fail to close after tapping (see p100). Wash the remaining mussels in cold water and clean them by pinching the stringy thread between your finger and thumb and firmly jerking it away from the mussel shell.

2 Season the chicken with salt and pepper. Heat the oil in a large, high-sided pan, and fry the chicken drumsticks over medium heat for about 8 minutes, until golden brown on all sides. Transfer to a bowl and set aside.

3 Add the onion and garlic to the same pan and sweat over medium heat for 3 minutes, stirring constantly. Add the rice and cook for 2 minutes before deglazing with the wine. Dissolve the stock and saffron in the hot water and add to the pan. Add the bay leaves and chicken drumsticks, cover with a lid, and cook over low heat for 10 minutes.

4 Add the mussels and strips of pepper to the pan, stir, and replace the lid. Cook for a further 5 minutes, and then stir in the shrimp and peas, cover again, and cook for 5 minutes. Season to taste with salt and pepper and serve with the lemon quarters.

Serves 4
Preparation time about 35 minutes

Mussels in White Wine

4½lb (2kg) mussels
6 tbsp olive oil
2 garlic cloves, lightly crushed
4 onions, sliced into strips
1 leek, sliced lengthwise into thin strips
2 carrots, peeled and thinly sliced
4 celery stalks, thinly sliced
1 chile, seeded and finely chopped
5 sprigs of thyme
½ tsp salt and 2 pinches of freshly
    ground black pepper
1 cup white wine
bunch of flat-leaf parsley, leaves
    roughly chopped
baguette, to serve (optional)

1 Discard any damaged or open mussels that fail to close after tapping (see below). Wash the remaining mussels in cold water and clean them by pinching the stringy thread between your finger and thumb and firmly jerking it away from the mussel shell.

2 Heat the olive oil in a large pan with plenty of room for the vegetables and mussels. Sauté the garlic, onions, leek, carrots, celery, chile, and thyme over medium heat for 5 minutes. Season with the salt and pepper. Pour in the white wine and bring to a boil.

3 Add the mussels to the pan and cook, covered, over medium heat for 15 minutes.

4 Once the mussels are cooked, add the chopped parsley and stir. Serve the mussels with the vegetable and white wine broth. If available, a fresh baguette goes great with this.

The tap test
To test whether an open mussel is still alive and fresh, tap it gently on a hard surface. If the mussel closes up in response, it's alive and okay to eat. If it doesn't, then discard it.

Cod in an Herb Vegetable Broth

2 potatoes, peeled and chopped into
½in (1cm) cubes
1 small fennel bulb, stem removed, cut
into ¼in (6mm) strips
1 carrot, peeled, halved lengthwise, then
cut into ½in (1cm) thick pieces
2 celery stalks, cut into ½in (1cm) thick
pieces
1 small leek, sliced lengthwise then cut
into ¾in (2cm) wide strips
4 cups water
sprig of rosemary
2 sprigs of thyme
3 sprigs of lemon balm
1 garlic clove, lightly crushed
10oz (300g) cod fillet (or another type of
fish), sliced into 1½in (3cm) wide pieces
salt and freshly ground black pepper
½ bunch of flat-leaf parsley, leaves finely
chopped, to garnish
2 tbsp olive oil, to garnish

1 Put the vegetables into a pan and cover with the water. Bring to a boil over high heat, and then cover and leave to simmer over low heat for about 8 minutes. Add the rosemary, thyme, and lemon balm to the pan along with the garlic.

2 Add the fish to the pan and mix gently with the vegetables. Poach, uncovered, in the broth for about 8 minutes, until cooked. Season to taste with salt and pepper. Remove the sprigs of herbs, serve the stew on 2 deep plates, and garnish each portion with the chopped parsley and 1 tablespoon of oil.

Bannock Bread Alsace Style

4 radishes, thinly sliced
bunch of chives, sliced into small rings
2 cups all-purpose flour, plus extra
   for dusting
1 tsp baking powder
5½oz (150g) bacon, cut into small cubes
½ tsp salt
1 cup water
4 tbsp sour cream

1 Mix the radishes and chives together in a bowl and set these aside while you make the dough.

2 Combine the flour, baking powder, bacon, and salt in a bowl. Make a well in the center and pour in the water. Use your fingers to work the flour gradually in to the water from the edge. As soon as the mixture comes together, knead it vigorously by hand until you have a supple dough.

3 Halve the dough and shape it into 2 balls. Press the balls flat on a floured work surface and pull out the edges with your hands until the flatbreads are the same size as the base of your pan. Cook each one in turn in a nonstick pan, without oil, over medium heat for about 6 minutes on each side, turning regularly. Spread each of the cooked breads with 2 tablespoons of sour cream and sprinkle with the chopped chives and radishes.

Who's the boss?

Do you find that sometimes your dough is too firm and other times too sticky, depending on its mood? Don't worry, this has nothing to do with inadequate baking skills. Every variety of flour behaves a bit differently. Just show the dough who is in charge: to get the perfect consistency, you may need to add a bit more water or flour than specified in the recipe.

For 2 people
Preparation time about 30 minutes · proving time 1 hour
· baking time about 35 minutes

Bread Rolls from a Pan

5 tbsp milk
1 tbsp butter
1 tbsp sugar
1 tsp salt
2 tsp dried yeast
1 egg
2 cups all-purpose flour, plus 2 tbsp
   for dusting

1 Put the milk, butter, sugar, and salt into a pan and heat until the butter has melted. Transfer to a bowl and let cool for 5 minutes, and then stir in the yeast until it has dissolved. Let stand for about 10 minutes, until the yeast starts to bubble. Add the egg and stir until smooth. Gradually mix in the flour until you have a stiff dough. Dust the dough with the 2 tablespoons of flour and knead it until it is supple. Cover and let prove in a warm place for 1 hour.

2 Divide the dough into 4 equal-sized portions and shape these into balls on a lightly floured work surface.

3 Heat a nonstick pan without any oil. Add the dough balls to the pan and cover with a lid. Bake at medium heat for 1 minute then reduce the temperature and continue cooking over low heat for a further 5 minutes.

4 Turn the rolls and continue cooking for another 8 minutes over low heat, and then turn again and bake for a further 8 minutes. Turn the rolls once more, switch off the stove, and leave the rolls resting in the closed pan for 10 minutes.

All together now: cheeeeese!
If you've bought cheese from a deli counter to have with your bread rolls, make sure different cheese varieties are kept separated from each other. Wrap each cheese in foil then make tiny holes in the foil to allow the cheese to breathe—unless the cheese is particularly smelly, in which case the foil is best left intact.

Stuffed Flatbreads

2 cups all-purpose flour, plus extra
  for dusting
¼ tsp baking powder
salt and freshly ground black pepper
¾ cup water
1¾oz (50g) salami, cut into small cubes
1¾oz (50g) Gouda cheese, coarsely grated
2 tbsp canola oil

1 Mix the flour and baking powder and a pinch each of salt and pepper in a bowl. Make a well in the center of the flour and add the water. Gradually stir the flour into the water until the mixture forms a stiff dough, and then continue to knead the dough until it is supple.

2 Split the dough into 4 equal-sized portions. Shape these into balls then use a rolling pin to roll them out on a floured work surface into discs measuring about 6in (15cm) in diameter. Alternatively, mold them into shape with the ball of your hand.

3 Top half the dough circles with salami and cheese. Fold the other dough halves over the top and press the edges together firmly with the prongs of a fork.

4 Heat the oil in a pan and cook the flatbreads on each side over medium heat, with the pan covered, for about 5 minutes, turning two or three times during this process.

Beach paradise
Camping on the beach is so romantic—lying in your tent at night listening to the waves lapping is an unforgettable experience. To make sure it really is paradise, pitch your tent on soft sand. And don't forget to check the high tide mark—you must know how high the water could come in extreme circumstances. In some places, you can even rent a beach hammock and sleep under the star-studded sky. What a dream!

Pan-Cooked Apple Cake

2 tart apples, peeled, cored, and thinly sliced
1 cup sugar, plus 2 tbsp
1 tbsp oil
zest and juice of ½ lemon
10 tbsp soft butter
3 eggs
2 cups all-purpose flour
2 tsp cocoa powder
2 tsp baking powder
½ tsp ground cinnamon
1 tbsp confectioner's sugar

1 Put the apples in a pan (10½in/26cm diameter) with the 2 tablespoons of sugar and the oil and lemon juice, and cook over medium heat for 8 minutes, stirring occasionally to prevent the apples from burning.

2 Meanwhile, add the butter, cup of sugar, eggs, and lemon zest to a bowl and stir until well combined. Combine the flour, cocoa powder, baking powder, and cinnamon and stir in to the butter, sugar, and egg mixture. Spread the mixture over the apples, smooth the surface, and cover the pan with a lid. Bake over medium heat for 5 minutes, and then continue cooking over the lowest heat for about another 20 minutes until the cake is cooked.

3 Turn the cake out of the pan using a plate to help, let cool slightly, dust with confectioner's sugar, and serve.

For 4 people · preparation time about 25 minutes

French Toast with Coconut and Mango Salad

For the mango salad
2 mangoes, pit removed, and cut into
⅛in (3mm) thick slices
1 tbsp lemon juice
2 tbsp honey
4 tbsp coconut milk

For the strips of bread
14oz (400g) day-old bread
1 cup condensed milk
1 cup shredded coconut

1 Put the mangoes in a bowl with the lemon juice, honey, and coconut milk. Combine the ingredients well then set aside.

2 To make the toast sticks, cut the bread into ¾in (2cm) thick slices and then into ¾in (2cm) wide strips. Put the condensed milk and shredded coconut into two deep dishes. Turn the strips of bread first in the condensed milk then in the coconut. Toast over medium heat until golden—you can do this on a grill or on a gas stove using a nonstick pan without oil. Serve the toast with the mango salad.

Fire it up

Feel the warm wind on your skin and the smell of the barbecue in your nostrils as the fire crackles, sizzles, and spits. Yes, it's summer! That open-air feeling plus a barbecue go hand in hand. So don't delay; get grilling!

Barbecue enthusiasts like to get their food fired up over a charcoal grill and swear by the fabulous and unique flavor this imparts. But charcoal barbecues are prohibited for safety reasons on some campsites due to the increased risk of fire caused by flying sparks, so some campers settle for a gas-powered option from the outset. And there's no reason to be disappointed—a gas barbecue has plenty of benefits: it's easy to operate, it heats up in no time, it's no trouble to clean, and the fuel is usually readily available.

Firing up

When barbecuing with charcoal, use special barbecue lighters (eco-friendly options are available) or appropriate natural alternatives. Gasoline and other chemical substances are a fire hazard, so please steer clear of these! If you are using a gas barbecue, to light it up: open the lid and the valve on the gas cylinder, ignite the burners, set them to the highest level, close the lid, and wait for about 10 minutes.

Hot enough?

A charcoal barbecue takes around 30 minutes to heat up. Charcoal is the right choice for brisk, brief barbecuing, but if you want your barbecue to last all evening, use briquettes since they are more durable. So when can you start cooking? If your barbecue doesn't have an integrated thermometer, use this trick to help. Hold the palm of your hand at roughly beer bottle height above the grill. If you need to pull it away after 4 seconds, the barbecue is at a high enough heat (450°F/230°C or above) for steaks. If you can withstand 5–7 seconds, a medium heat has been reached (347°F/175°C or above), the optimum temperature for fish. And if you can last 8–10 seconds, you can barbecue delicate foods such as vegetables at a lower heat (248°F/120°C or above). Ideally, cook with the lid closed so your food is enveloped by heat and aroma from all sides.

Top 5 barbecue accessories

1. Barbecue tongs for turning meat, fish, and vegetables
2. A grill tray or aluminum foil for vegetables and other small items
3. Meat thermometer for testing
4. Grill brush to clean the barbecue
5. Silicon brush for oiling and marinating

Grilling options

Do you know the difference between direct and indirect grilling?

Direct grilling: the food is positioned above the embers or the burner. This is ideal for searing steaks or hamburgers, for example.

Indirect grilling: you slide the embers to the side or switch off the burner so the food isn't above direct heat. This is good for slow cooking meat such as spareribs. We also recommend cooking directly first above the flames then finishing off with indirect heat until done.

Skewer it up!

We just love barbecuing with skewers! But metal skewers get hot very quickly and have to be handled using gloves, so we usually use the wooden variety in our recipes. Soak the skewers in water for at least 30 minutes before you add the ingredients to avoid them burning on the barbecue. If you have a freezer compartment in your RV or motor home, soaked wooden skewers can be frozen and don't need to be reimmersed in water before use.

BBQ Chicken in Orange Marinade

For the chicken

3 tbsp orange marmalade
4 tbsp BBQ sauce (store-bought or
  homemade, see recipe p16)
2 tbsp soy sauce
4 chicken breast fillets (5½ oz/150g each)

For the vegetables

3 red peppers, seeded and cut into
  1½in (4cm) cubes
2 red onions, cut into thick strips
1 tbsp olive oil
1 tbsp honey
salt and freshly ground black pepper

Also

8 pieces aluminum foil (12 x 12in/
  30 × 30cm each)

1 Stir the marmalade, BBQ sauce, and soy sauce in a bowl and marinate the chicken breast for at least 1 hour, or ideally overnight.

2 Put the peppers and onions into a large bowl with the oil and honey. Season with 1 teaspoon of salt and a pinch of pepper and mix well. Lay a piece of aluminum foil on top of another then repeat with the rest of the foil pieces to create 4 thick foil sheets. Divide the vegetable mixture evenly between them, spreading it in the center of each sheet. Fold up the foil and scrunch the open sides together to seal the packages.

3 Remove the chicken breast from the marinade, season with some salt and pepper, and grill on each side over medium heat for 5 minutes. At the same time, lay the pepper packages on the grill and cook over medium heat for 10 minutes, turning occasionally to make sure the vegetables cook evenly. Remove from the grill and leave to rest for 5 minutes. Divide between 4 plates and serve along with the chicken breast.

4 This dish can also be cooked in a pan on a gas stove. To do this, heat 1 tablespoon of canola oil in a pan. Fry the chicken breast over medium heat for 5 minutes on each side. Meanwhile, heat 1 tablespoon of canola oil in a separate pan and cook the vegetables over medium heat for about 10 minutes, stirring occasionally.

One-pan power

You may be wondering how many pans you need while camping. One pan at least is definitely helpful, allowing you to make a range of dishes so you're not always cooking the same thing. Otherwise, the number of pans you take will depend on how many people you are cooking for and how you are traveling. A backpacker might take a single pan while a family in a motor home has room for at least a few different-sized pans.

For 4 people
Preparation time about 40 minutes

Stuffed Steaks on a Ratatouille and Carrot Base

For the steaks

4 steaks (5½oz/150g each), your choice
  of beef, pork, veal, or turkey
4 tsp medium–hot mustard
4 slices prosciutto
2 sprigs of sage leaves
salt and freshly ground black pepper

For the vegetables

3 tbsp olive oil
2 carrots, peeled, quartered, then sliced
  diagonally into ¼in (6mm) pieces
4 potatoes, peeled, quartered, then sliced
  diagonally into ¼in (6mm) pieces
1 small eggplant, chopped into ¾in (2cm)
  cubes
1 zucchini, chopped into ¾in (2cm) cubes
1 red pepper, seeded and chopped into
  ¾in (2cm) cubes
2 tomatoes, chopped into ¾in (2cm) cubes
7oz (200g) can chopped tomatoes
1 tbsp sugar
1 tbsp herbes de Provence

1 Use a knife to cut a pocket in each steak and smear the inside of each with 1 teaspoon of mustard. Spread out the prosciutto, lay the sage leaves evenly on top, and roll the slices up. Stuff 1 little proscuitto roll into the pocket in each steak.

2 For the vegetables, put a pan (without any plastic handles) on the grill. Heat the oil in the pan and sauté the vegetables over medium heat for 5 minutes. Stir in the canned tomatoes, sugar, and herbs. Cover and simmer for 12 minutes, stirring occasionally.

4 Season the steaks with salt and pepper and grill them on the barbecue or fry them in a pan over high heat for about 4 minutes each side. Season the vegetables to taste with salt and pepper and divide between 4 plates. Top the vegetables with the cooked steaks and serve.

For 4 people
Preparation time about 30 minutes

Barbecued Herb Camembert

1 garlic clove, finely chopped or crushed
1 tbsp olive oil
8 bay leaves
8 sprigs of rosemary
8 sprigs of thyme
8 sprigs of oregano
4 Camembert cheese rounds
bread or baguette, to serve

Also
4 pieces of kitchen twine, 24in (60cm) each

1 Stir the garlic into the olive oil. Arrange 1 bay leaf and 1 sprig each of rosemary, thyme, and oregano underneath and on top of each Camembert. Tie each one up into a little package using kitchen twine.

2 Drizzle the herb Camemberts with the garlic oil and barbecue over medium heat for about 4 minutes on each side. Take care to avoid letting the cheese burn or melt onto the barbecue. The herbs can burn as they won't be eaten.

3 The cheese is ready when it has begun to brown slightly and small blisters are forming on the surface. Arrange the Camembert cheese rounds on 4 plates, snip off the kitchen twine, and remove the herbs. Serve with fresh bread or a baguette.

Red onion confit from the pantry
These cheeses go wonderfully with a red onion confit, which you can make at home and take with you in a jar, as you would with jam. To make the confit, peel 8 red onions and slice in half and then into thin strips. Caramelize 1 tbsp sugar in a pan, remove briefly from the stove, add 2 tbsp butter, let it foam and immediately add the onions and stir. Sweat for about a minute then deglaze with ½ cup grape juice and 2 tbsp balsamic vinegar. Add 2 cloves, 1 bay leaf, and 2 juniper berries, cover, and braise over low heat for about 20 minutes, stirring occasionally. Then remove the lid and simmer over medium heat until the liquid has boiled down to create a syrupy consistency. Season to taste with salt and freshly ground black pepper and pour into screw-top jars while still hot. Sealed, this will keep unrefrigerated for up to 2 weeks.

For 4 x 6¼oz (180g) steaks
Preparation time abnout 10 minutes

Three Tenderizing Steak Marinades

For the yogurt and curry marinade
½ cup full-fat yogurt
1 garlic clove, finely chopped or crushed
1 tbsp lemon juice
1 tsp medium–hot mustard
1 tbsp curry powder
1 tsp salt
4 tbsp canola oil

For the paprika and mustard marinade
1 small onion, finely diced
2 tbsp whole-grain Dijon mustard
½ cup apple juice
1 tbsp lemon juice
1 tbsp paprika
1 tsp dried thyme
1 tsp salt
4 tbsp canola oil

For the honey and chile marinade
2 red chiles, seeded and finely chopped
1 garlic clove, finely chopped or crushed
2 tbsp white balsamic vinegar
2 tbsp honey
1 tsp medium–hot mustard
1 tsp dried rosemary
1 tsp salt
8 tbsp canola oil

1 To make the yogurt and curry marinade, stir the yogurt, garlic, lemon juice, mustard, curry powder, and salt together in a bowl until the salt has dissolved. Pour in the oil, stir, then add the meat.

2 For the paprika and mustard marinade, place the onion in a bowl. Add all the remaining ingredients, apart from the oil, and stir until the salt has dissolved. Pour in the oil, stir, then add the meat.

3 For the honey and chile marinade, place the chiles and garlic in a bowl then add the vinegar, honey, mustard, rosemary, and salt, and stir everything until the salt has dissolved. Pour in the oil, stir, then add the meat.

Marinating made easy
Ideally meat should be marinated for 2 hours or overnight in freezer bags in the fridge to allow the flavors to blend perfectly. Cuts of meat such as ribeye, porterhouse, T-bone, fillet steak, or sirloin are naturally very tender, moist, and full of flavor, so they also taste fantastic simply seasoned with salt and pepper.

 For 4 people · preparation time about 45 minutes · marinating time 2 hours

Grilled Corn on the Cob

4 fresh corn cobs
juice of 1 lime
6 tbsp maple syrup
2 tbsp soy sauce
1 tbsp chili powder

Also
8 toothpicks

1 Parboil the corn cobs in plenty of salted water for 10 minutes. Meanwhile, mix the lime juice with the maple syrup, soy sauce, and chili powder. Place the corn in the marinade and leave to infuse for 2 hours, turning occasionally.

2 Grill the corn on the barbecue over medium heat until golden brown all over. Then brush liberally with the marinade. To serve, insert a toothpick at each end of the cooked corn cobs.

 Delicious festival food
No one wants to leave a festival to go to the supermarket. Before you get there, think about what you would like to eat and pack all the essentials. You can keep it quite simple: just toss a steak or a couple of sausages on the barbecue to go with the grilled corn on the cob, and the partygoers will be full and happy before you know it.

Grilled Cherry Tomato Kebabs

3 sausages (about 14oz/400g)
1 onion, finely diced
1 tsp mustard
1 egg
3 tbsp white bread crumbs
32 cherry tomatoes (or 16 cherry
 tomatoes and 8 small peppers,
 seeded and halved)
1 tbsp canola oil
salt and freshly ground black pepper

Also
8 wooden skewers, 8in/20cm long

1 Soak the wooden skewers for at least 30 minutes in water. Slice the sausages in half lengthwise, press out the sausage meat, and put it in a bowl. Add the onion and mix it in along with the mustard, egg, and white bread crumbs. Work everything together to create a consistent mixture and shape into 32 similar-sized balls.

2 On each wooden skewer, alternate 4 cherry tomatoes or 4 pepper halves and 4 meatballs. Before cooking, brush with a little oil and season with salt and pepper.

3 Cook on the barbecue or fry in a pan over medium heat for about 8 minutes, turning occasionally to cook both sides.

For 4 people
Preparation time about 35 minutes

Hot Dogs Wrapped in Bacon

For the sauerkraut salad

7oz (200g) sauerkraut
1 small pineapple, cored, flesh removed,
   roughly grated
3½ tbsp pineapple juice
2 tsp honey
1 tbsp canola oil
2 tbsp full-fat yogurt
salt and freshly ground black pepper

For the hot dogs

2 slices Emmental cheese
8 hot dogs
16 slices of bacon
8 hot dog buns
8 tbsp remoulade sauce

1 Pour the sauerkraut into a colander, rinse, and leave to drain. Transfer to a bowl and toss through with a fork.

2 Add the pineapple to the sauerkraut. Add the pineapple juice, honey, oil, and yogurt and mix well. Season to taste with salt and pepper and set aside.

3 To make the hot dogs, slice the cheese into ¼in (6mm) wide strips. Make a lengthwise incision in the hot dogs, but don't cut them all the way through. Insert the cheese into this incision and wrap each hot dog in 2 slices of bacon. Grill on the barbecue over medium heat until the bacon is crispy. Toast the hot dog buns, cut side down, for about 10 seconds.

4 Fill each bun with some of the sauerkraut salad and top with a hot dog. Garnish each hot dog with 1 tablespoon of the remoulade sauce and serve.

For 4 people
Preparation time about 40 minutes

BBQ Goulash

14oz (400g) sirloin, cut into ½in (1cm)
　wide strips
1 cup BBQ sauce (store-bought or
　homemade, see recipe p16)
14oz (400g) potatoes, peeled and cut
　into large chunks
2 onions, halved, stems removed, then
　sliced lengthwise into strips
1 green pepper, seeded and diced
1 red chile, seeded and diced
10oz (300g) green beans, cut into
　1½in (4cm) strips

Also
8 pieces aluminum foil (12 x 12in/
　30 × 30cm each)

1　Mix together the sirloin strips and the BBQ sauce in a large bowl. Put the potatoes, onion, green pepper, chile, and green beans in the bowl and mix with the sirloin and sauce.

2　Lay a piece of aluminum foil on top of another and repeat with the rest of the foil pieces to create 4 thick foil sheets. Divide the meat mixture evenly between them, spreading it in the center of each sheet. Fold the foil over the mixture, then scrunch the edges together—not too tightly, you need to leave a bit of room.

3　Put the packages on the grill and cook over medium heat, turning occasionally, for about 25 minutes. Serve straight from the packages or dish up on 4 plates.

Prepping ahead for the barbecue
This dish is great when prepared in advance and tastes even better the longer the flavors have to develop. You can also cook it in a large pan on a gas stove. Heat 2 tbsp canola oil and sauté all the ingredients over medium heat for about 20 minutes. Stir as frequently as possible to avoid it catching on fire.

For 4 people
Preparation time about 50 minutes

Potato Gratin Cooked on a Camping BBQ

8 waxy potatoes, washed, peel on, cut into
¼in (6mm) thick slices
1 large onion, halved then cut into thin strips
1 garlic clove, finely chopped or crushed
5½oz (150g) Gouda cheese (or Cheddar or
Raclette), roughly grated
2–3 pinches of grated nutmeg
salt and freshly ground black pepper
4 tbsp butter

Also

8 pieces aluminum foil (12 x 12in/
30 × 30cm each)

1 Wash the potatoes very thoroughly before slicing them. Put the potatoes, onion, garlic, and cheese into a large bowl. Season with the nutmeg, 1 teaspoon of salt, and a pinch of pepper and mix everything well.

2 Lay a piece of aluminum foil on top of another then repeat with the rest of the pieces to create 4 thick foil sheets. Divide the potato mixture evenly between them, spreading it in the center of each sheet. Top each potato package with 1 tbsp butter and fold up the foil, scrunching together the open sides to seal the packages.

3 Place the packages on the grill and cook over medium heat for 35 minutes, turning the packages every 10 minutes during the cooking time to make sure the potatoes cook evenly. Remove from the barbecue, let rest for 5 minutes, and serve straight out of the foil packages.

When potatoes travel ...

Potatoes don't like the light, so they should be stored in a cool, dark place—a dark cabinet is usually the perfect location. When you're traveling, for example in an RV, and need to find an alternative storage solution for your potatoes, just wrap them, unwashed, in newspaper!

Makes 4
Preparation time about 1 hour 30 minutes
· proving time 1 hour 30 minutes

Mini Pan-Cooked Flatbreads

¼ oz (7g) packet active dried yeast
1 tbsp honey
1½ cup warm water, divided
2 tsp salt
4½ cups all-purpose flour, plus extra
    for dusting
2 tbsp olive oil
2 tsp black caraway seeds

1 Stir together the yeast, honey, and 3½ tablespoons of warm water in a bowl until the yeast has dissolved. Leave to stand for about 10 minutes until the yeast starts to bubble. Combine the salt and flour in a large bowl. Add the yeast mixture, olive oil, and 1⅓ cups warm water.

2 Knead everything together by hand, then continue to work the dough for 5 minutes on a floured work surface. The dough should come together to form a ball and no longer stick to your hands. If necessary, add a little more flour to achieve the desired consistency. Return the dough to the bowl, cover, and leave to prove in a warm place for about 1 hour.

3 Remove the dough from the bowl, knead it briefly again on the lightly floured work surface, and divide into 4 equal-sized pieces. Shape the pieces of dough into balls, then press them with the palm of your hand to create roughly ½in (1cm) thick flatbreads. Scatter the black caraway seeds on top, cover, and leave to prove for a further 30 minutes.

4 Cook the flatbreads in batches on the barbecue over medium to high heat for 6–7 minutes on each side. Close the barbecue during cooking (or you can place a saucepan lid over the flatbreads). Remove from the barbecue and wrap in a kitchen towel to keep the bread warm until all the flatbreads have been cooked. Serve warm as a side dish.

In a pan
These flatbreads can also be cooked in a pan on a gas stove (see photo). Heat a nonstick pan without any oil or fat and cook the flatbreads, covered, in the pan over medium to low heat for 6–7 minutes on each side.

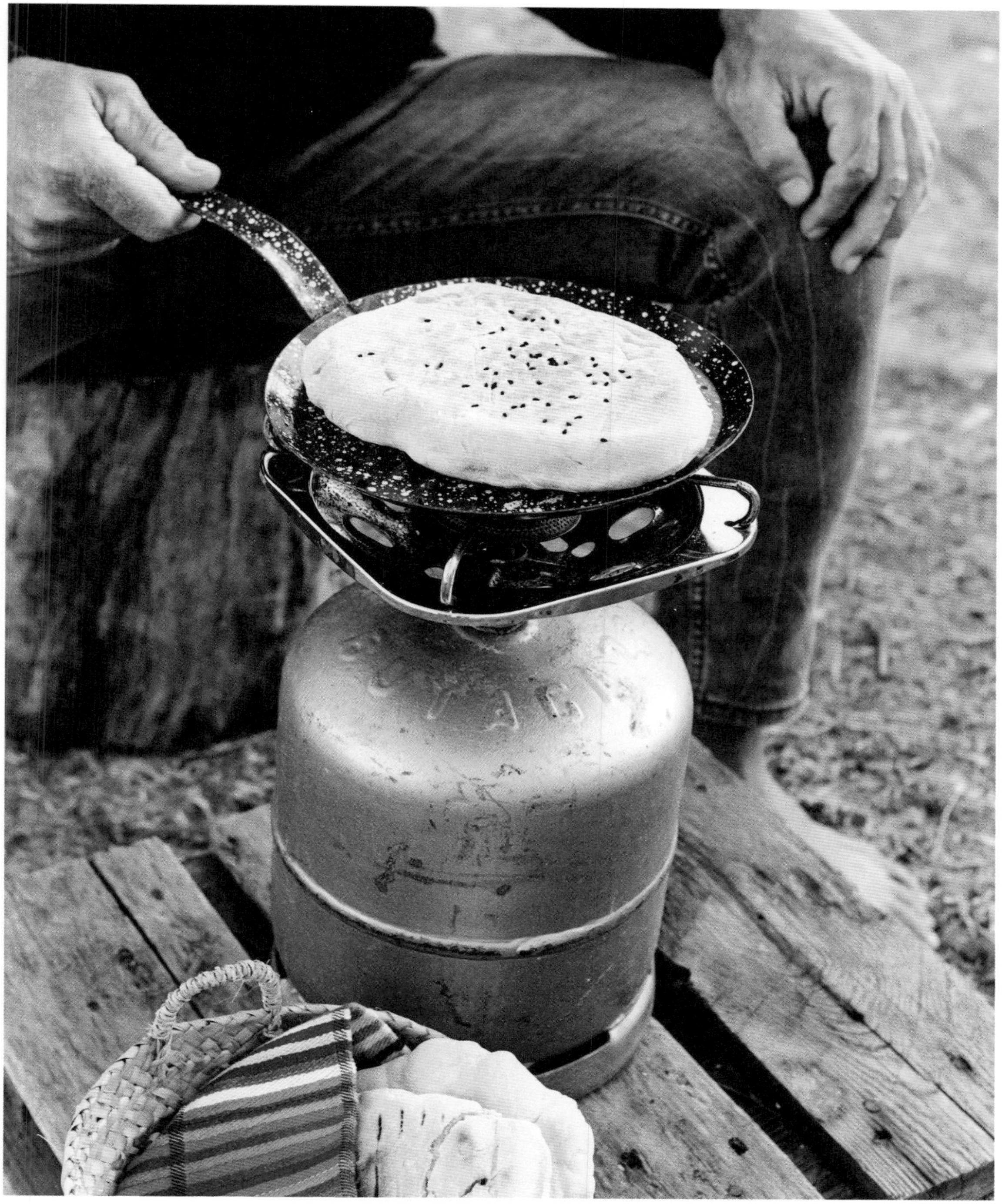

For 4 people
Preparation time about 45 minutes · marinating time about 30 minutes

Pan-Fried Pork and Beef with Mediterranean Vegetables

9oz (250g) pork fillets
9oz (250g) rump steak
1 tbsp tomato puree
1 tbsp soy sauce
1 zucchini, cut into ½in (1cm) chunks
8 cherry tomatoes, halved
1 small eggplant, sliced lengthwise then cut
   into ½in (1cm) thick strips
1 small fennel bulb, stem removed and cut
   into ¼in (6mm) wide strips
1 red onion, cut into 8 wedges
4 tbsp olive oil
2 tsp herbes de Provence
salt and freshly ground black pepper
4 tbsp sour cream, to serve

Also
8 pieces aluminum foil (12 x 12in/
   30 × 30cm each)

1 Before cutting up the meat, remove any excess fat or tendons. Marinate the pork and steak in a bowl with the tomato puree and soy sauce for about 30 minutes.

2 Meanwhile, put the zucchini, cherry tomatoes, eggplant, fennel, and onion in a bowl and mix with the oil, herbes de Provence, 1 teaspoon of salt, and a pinch of pepper. Add the meat with the marinade and mix everything together thoroughly.

3 Lay a piece of aluminum foil on top of another then repeat with the rest of the foil pieces to create 4 thick foil sheets. Divide the meat and vegetable mixture evenly between them, spreading it out in the center of each sheet. Fold up the foil and scrunch the open sides together to seal your vegetable packages.

4 Put packages onto the grill and cook over medium heat for about 25 minutes. Turn the packages occasionally to make sure everything cooks evenly. Remove from the grill and let rest for 5 minutes. Open the foil and serve straight from the foil, topping each package with 1 tablespoon sour cream.

On the stove!
This dish can also be prepared in a pan (see photo). Heat 2 tbsp canola oil and fry the strips of meat and vegetables over medium heat for about 20 minutes, stirring occasionally.

Crazy about campfires?

Holding a stick with a piece of dough on the end over the campfire and watching it slowly color is something that always reminds us of our childhood camping trips and that feeling of impatience that the bread would just never be ready. Those experiences, which fascinated us then, are still a real pleasure today. When people gather around a campfire, their mood lifts immediately. It brings out the romantic in everyone–so let those sparks fly. Our recipes for campfire bread on a stick are irresistible!

Top 10 hottest campfire to-do list

You must try these 10 campfire suggestions at least once in your life:

1. Tell a ghost story.
2. Munch on toasted marshmallows.
3. Explain a natural phenomenon to the kids.
4. Sing a classic campfire song, such as "American Pie" by Don McLean or "Wonderwall" by Oasis.
5. Play one of the above songs on a guitar–or applaud someone else who can.
6. Eat a potato that has been cooked in the embers.
7. Collect wood for yourself (at least one piece) and add it to the fire.
8. Sit as quietly as a mouse and listen to the fire crackling and sizzling.
9. Entrust a friend with a genuine secret.
10. Dance like nobody's watching!

For 4 people
Preparation time about 1 hour · proofing time about 1 hour 10 minutes

Stick-Bread Options

For the basic dough

¼ oz (7g) packet active dried yeast
1 tbsp sugar
1 tsp salt
1 cup warm water
2 tbsp olive oil
3 cups all-purpose flour, plus extra
   for dusting

For the herb stick bread

2 garlic cloves, finely chopped or crushed
4 sprigs of flat-leaf parsley, leaves and
   stalks finely chopped
bunch of chives, chopped into small rings

For the onion stick bread

1 cup fried onions
1 tsp paprika

For the ham and cheese stick bread

1 cup diced ham
1 cup grated Gouda cheese

Also

4 roasting sticks (each measuring about
   20in/50cm)

1 To make the dough, stir the yeast, sugar, salt, and water in a bowl until the yeast has dissolved. Leave to stand for about 10 minutes until the yeast starts to bubble. Stir in the olive oil and gradually add enough flour to create a stiff dough. Add the remaining flour then knead by hand until the dough is supple. Choose one of the five bread versions below, or go directly to step 5.

2 For the herb stick bread, add the garlic, parsley, and chives to the dough and knead until well combined.

3 For the onion stick bread, knead the fried onions and paprika into the dough.

4 For the ham and cheese stick bread, knead the ham and Gouda into the dough.

5 Leave the dough to proof for 1 hour. Wash the wooden sticks thoroughly with water and, if necessary, scrub them with a brush along the section where the bread dough will be wrapped.

6 Divide the dough into 4 equal-sized portions. Roll out each one by hand on a floured work surface to create a sausage shape about 20in (50cm) long. Wrap the lengths of dough around the prepared end of the sticks and either cook them over the embers of an open campfire, or over the glowing barbecue coals. Turn the wooden sticks frequently while cooking. Depending on the heat and distance from the embers, it will take 30–40 minutes for the bread to cook. The bread is ready when it is brown and crisp on the outside and gives a hollow sound when tapped.

For 4 people
Preparation time about 25 minutes · proving time about 1 hour 10 minutes

BBQ Pizza

For the dough

¼ oz (7g) packet active dried yeast
1 tsp sugar
½ tsp salt
¾ cup warm water
1 tbsp olive oil
3 cups all-purpose flour, plus extra
    for dusting

For the sauce

2 tbsp dried oregano
pinch of grated nutmeg
2 tbsp sugar
1½ cups tomato purée
salt

For the topping

2 balls of mozzarella
9oz (250g) Gouda cheese
8 slices of ham

1 To make the dough, stir the yeast, sugar, salt, and water in a bowl until the yeast has dissolved. Leave to stand for about 10 minutes until the yeast starts to bubble. Stir in the olive oil and gradually add enough flour to create a stiff dough. Add the remaining flour then knead by hand until the dough is supple. Cover and leave to prove in a warm place for 1 hour.

2 Meanwhile, for the sauce, stir the oregano, nutmeg, and sugar into the tomato puree and season to taste with salt. For the topping, drain the mozzarella and cut each ball into 8 slices. Roughly grate the Gouda and tear the ham into bite-sized pieces.

3 Divide the dough into 4 equal-sized portions and shape into balls. Roll these out on a floured work surface to about 8in (20cm) diameter using a rolling pin, or press into shape using your hands. Place the flatbreads in batches on the grill, immediately close the lid (or place a pan lid over the pizzas), and cook over medium heat for about 1 minute each side. Remove and spread evenly with the sauce, sprinkle over the Gouda, and top each with 4 slices of mozzarella. Divide the ham between the bases and cook the pizzas on the barbecue for a further 3–5 minutes with the lid closed.

4 Since the temperature of every barbecue is different, it is important to check the cooking progress every so often. Lift each pizza and check the color and consistency of the base. If the dough is getting too dark underneath or is in danger of burning, remove the pizza from the grill, reduce the temperature, and then continue cooking. The pizzas are ready when the base is crisp and the cheese has melted.

For 4 people
Preparation time about 30 minutes · soaking time about 30 minutes

Antipasti Veggie Kebabs BBQ Style

For the marinade
1 garlic clove, finely chopped or crushed
small handful of mint, leaves finely chopped
4 tbsp olive oil
zest and juice of ½ lemon
1 tsp dried oregano

For the veggie kebabs
14oz (400g) can artichoke hearts
1 zucchini, sliced lengthwise, then cut
   crosswise into 16 equal-sized pieces
8 shiitake mushrooms, halved
8 small peppers, seeded and halved
9oz (250g) halloumi cheese, sliced
   lengthwise then cut into 8 equal-sized
   cubes
salt and freshly ground black pepper

Also
8 wooden skewers (8in/20cm each)

1 Soak the wooden skewers for at least 30 minutes in water. To make the marinade, stir together the garlic, mint, oil, lemon zest, 2 tablespoons of lemon juice, and oregano in a bowl and set aside.

2 Drain the artichoke hearts in a colander, then slice in half. Slide the zucchini, mushrooms, peppers, and halloumi cheese chunks onto the wooden skewers so they are evenly distributed and season with salt and pepper. Barbecue over medium heat for 3–4 minutes on each side. Brush with the marinade and serve.

3 You can also make the kebabs on a gas stove. To do this, heat 1 tablespoon of the olive oil in a nonstick pan and fry the veggie kebabs over medium heat for 3–4 minutes on each side. Brush with the marinade and serve.

Spear with your fork
To juice a lemon without a squeezer requires some manual work! Slice the lemon in half and stick a fork into the flesh a few times—this will make it easy to squeeze the lemon by hand. Or to make it even easier, stick the fork in the center of the lemon, then move it up and down and presto ... the juice just flows out of its own accord.

For 4 people
Preparation time about 45 minutes · soaking time about 30 minutes

Cauliflower and Zucchini Kebabs with Almond Salsa

For the almond salsa

1 shallot, finely diced
1 garlic clove, finely chopped or crushed
3 tbsp capers, finely chopped
½ cup olive oil
¼ cup ground almonds
2 tbsp chopped flat-leaf parsley
1 tbsp chopped mint
1 tsp dried oregano
1 tsp grated lemon zest
3 tsp lemon juice
salt and freshly ground black pepper

For the kebabs

2 zucchinis, ends removed
1 cauliflower, cut into small florets
2 tbsp olive oil
salt

Also

8 wooden skewers (8in/20cm each)

1 Soak the wooden skewers for at least 30 minutes in water. To make the salsa, stir all the ingredients together in a bowl and season to taste with salt and pepper. Set aside.

2 Use a potato peeler to slice the zucchini into thin strips. Take 2 strips of zucchini, place one on top of the other, and roll them up. Slide the cauliflower florets and zucchini rolls onto the wooden skewers, alternating between the two. Brush evenly with the oil and season with salt.

3 Grill over medium heat for 10–12 minutes, turning frequently so the kebabs do not burn. Drizzle evenly with the salsa and serve.

4 You can also make the kebabs on a gas stove. To do this, heat 1 tablespoon of olive oil in a nonstick pan and fry the cauliflower kebabs over medium heat for 10–12 minutes on all sides.

Grilled Garden Vegetables

2 tbsp soft butter
1 garlic clove, crushed
3 waxy potatoes, chopped into ½in (1cm)
  pieces
3 carrots, peeled and cut into ¼in (6mm)
  discs
1 kohlrabi, cut crosswise into ¼in (6mm)
  slices
5½oz (150g) green beans
¼ tsp dried oregano
¼ tsp ground turmeric
salt and freshly ground black pepper

Also

8 pieces aluminum foil (12 x 12in/
  30 ×30cm each)

1 Melt the butter in a pan on the hot grill. Add the garlic and let it infuse in the butter for 1 minute. Put the potatoes, carrots, kohlrabi, green beans, oregano, and turmeric in a large bowl along with the butter. Season with ½ teaspoon of salt and a pinch of pepper and mix well.

2 Lay a piece of aluminum foil on top of another then repeat with the rest of the foil pieces to create 4 thick foil sheets. Divide the vegetable mixture evenly between them, spreading it out in the center of each sheet. Fold up the foil and scrunch the open sides together to seal the packages.

3 Put them on the grill and cook over medium heat for about 20 minutes. Turn the packages occasionally to make sure the vegetables cook evenly. Remove from the grill, leave to rest for 5 minutes, then serve in the foil.

For 4 people · preparation time about 30 minutes

Barbecued Balsamic Bean Packages

2 garlic cloves, crushed
2 tbsp olive oil
2 tsp Dijon mustard
2 tsp maple syrup
2 tbsp balsamic vinegar
salt
1lb 5oz (600g) green or yellow
  beans, halved
1 red pepper, deseeded, cut into
  ¼in (6mm) strips
1 yellow pepper deseeded, cut into
  ¼in (6mm) strips
¼ cup pine nuts

Also

8 pieces aluminum foil (12 x 12in/
  30 × 30cm each)

1 Put the garlic, oil, mustard, maple syrup, and balsamic vinegar into a large bowl and season with ½ teaspoon of salt. Stir in the beans and peppers until they are completely coated in the marinade.

2 Lay a piece of aluminum foil on top of another one then repeat with the rest of the foil pieces to create 4 thick foil sheets. Divide the beans evenly between them, spreading them out in the center of each sheet. Drizzle over the remaining marinade from the bowl. Sprinkle with the pine nuts, fold up the foil, and scrunch the open sides together to seal the packages.

3 Place on the barbecue and grill over medium heat for 10–12 minutes, turning frequently to prevent the beans from burning. Remove from the grill and let rest for 5 minutes then serve in the foil.

For 4 people · preparation time about 15 minutes
Soaking time about 30 minutes · marinating time about 2 hours

Shrimp and Lime Kebabs

1lb 5oz (600g) raw jumbo shrimp (about
  16–20 shrimp), peeled and heads removed
2 garlic cloves, finely chopped or crushed
1 jalapeño, seeded and finely chopped
3 sprigs cilantro, leaves and stalks finely
  chopped
4 tbsp olive oil
1 tbsp raw cane sugar
½ tsp smoked paprika
½ tsp ground cumin
salt and freshly ground black pepper
2 limes

Also
4 wooden skewers (8in/20cm each)

1 Soak the wooden skewers for at least 30 minutes in water. Put the shrimp in a bowl and add all the ingredients except the lime. Cover and marinate in a cool place for at least 2 hours.

2 Trim the ends off 1 lime and slice into ¼in (6mm) thick rounds. Cut the second lime lengthwise into quarters and set aside. Slide the shrimp and lime slices onto the skewers, alternating with 1 shrimp and 1 lime. You should end up with 4–5 shrimp on each skewer.

3 Barbecue the shrimp kebabs over medium heat on each side for 3–4 minutes and serve with a lime segment.

4 You can also make the kebabs on a gas stove. To do this, heat 1 tablespoon of olive oil in a nonstick pan and fry the lime kebabs over medium heat for 3–4 minutes on each side. Serve each one with a quarter lime segment.

Pantry marinade
You can prepare the marinade while you are still at home. Crush all the ingredients except the oil using a pestle and mortar until you have a fine paste. Add the oil, mix everything well, transfer to a small, sterilized bottle, and seal. Alternatively, put all the marinade ingredients into a blender beaker and purée with a handheld blender until smooth, then decant into your container. The marinade will keep unrefrigerated for up to 1 week.

For 4 people
Preparation time about 40 minutes

Salmon in Foil with Spiced Cauliflower

2 tbsp butter
1 onion, finely diced
1 tsp ground ginger
1 tsp garlic granules
1 tsp chili flakes
2 tsp paprika
2 tsp ground coriander
½ tsp ground cumin
14oz (400g) can chopped tomatoes
1 small cauliflower, cut into florets
salt and freshly ground black pepper
4 salmon fillets (5½oz/150g each)

Also
8 pieces aluminum foil (12 x 12in/
   30 × 30cm each)

1 Heat the butter in a pan on the barbecue or on a gas stove. Fry the onion over medium heat for about 5 minutes until golden yellow. Add the ginger, garlic, chili flakes, paprika, coriander, and cumin and continue cooking for 2 minutes.

2 Add the chopped tomatoes and cauliflower florets and simmer for 8 minutes, stirring occasionally. Season to taste with salt. Remove the pan from the heat, set aside, and let cool for 10 minutes. Season the salmon with salt and pepper.

3 Lay one piece of aluminum foil on top of another and repeat with the rest of the foil pieces to create 4 thick foil sheets. Divide half of the cauliflower mixture evenly between them, spreading it in the center of each sheet. Place the fish fillets on top and cover with the remaining cauliflower. Fold up the foil and scrunch the open sides together to seal your packages.

4 Put packages onto the grill and cook over medium heat for about 20 minutes, turning every 5 minutes. Remove the packages from the grill and transfer to 4 plates, opening them up only when you are ready to serve.

Barbecued Sea Bass

2¼in (6cm) piece ginger, peeled
2 garlic cloves
2 sticks of lemongrass, sliced into ¾in (2cm)
  chunks
1 red chile, seeded
4 sprigs of mint, leaves and stalks chopped
piece of star anise
4 cleaned sea bass (10oz/300g each)
salt and freshly ground black pepper
4 limes, or lemons, cut into 8 slices

Also
2 old newspapers
4 pieces of kitchen twine (15½in/40cm each)

1 Roughly crush the ginger, garlic, lemongrass, chile, mint, and star anise in a pestle and mortar or chop with a knife. Season the fish with salt and pepper, including inside the cavity. Distribute the spice mix evenly between the fish, inserting it into the cavity in each one.

2 Lay out the newspaper in 5 equal layers and moisten with a bit of water. Place 4 slices of lime in a row in the center of each paper stack and place the fish on top, then add the remaining lime slices. Roll up the newspaper firmly and tie each package with kitchen twine. Cover the fish packages completely with salted water and leave to soak for 15 minutes.

3 Grill the fish on the barbecue over medium heat for about 15 minutes on each side. To serve, unwrap the fish from the newspaper, remove the herbs and spices from the cavity, and arrange on 4 plates.

Fish ahoy!
There are several ways to cook a whole fish over the campfire and this is a fantastic way to cook fish! You can wrap the fish in aluminum foil and place it in the hot embers. Fish with firm flesh can be put on a skewer held over the coals. Or use a piece of professional grilling equipment: a BBQ fish grill holds the fish and makes turning it really easy (see photo).

Lemony Salmon with Sesame Seeds

2 lemons, juice reserved
1 garlic clove, finely chopped or pressed
2 tbsp olive oil
3 tbsp chopped dill
1 tbsp chopped flat-leaf parsley
2 tsp Dijon mustard
1 tsp Worcestershire sauce
1lb 5oz (600g) salmon fillet, cut into
   1½in (4cm) chunks
2 tbsp sesame seeds
¼ tsp chili flakes

Also

8 wooden, or metal, skewers
   (8in/20cm each)

1 If using wooden skewers, soak these for at least 30 minutes in water. Chop a generous chunk off the ends of the lemons and squeeze them by hand, then slice the lemons into ¼in (6mm) thick slices. Combine the garlic, lemon juice, oil, dill, parsley, mustard, and Worcestershire sauce in a bowl and set aside.

2 To make the kebabs, hold 2 skewers about ½in (1cm) apart. Slide alternating pieces of salmon and folded slices of lemon onto the skewers. Continue in the same manner with the remaining 6 skewers.

3 Brush the salmon kebabs evenly with the herb and mustard mixture. Mix the sesame seeds and chili flakes together and scatter all over the salmon kebabs. Grill on the barbecue over medium heat for 2 minutes each side then serve.

4 You can also cook the kebabs on a gas stove. To do this, heat 1 tablespoon of olive oil in a nonstick pan and fry the salmon kebabs over medium heat for 2 minutes on each side. Serve each kebab with a quarter lemon segment.

Green fingers

If you have managed to get ahold of some fresh herbs, once they have been washed and shaken dry, they will keep best chilled—either in a storage container or in a resealable freezer bag that you have blown air into.

For 4 people
Preparation time about 20 minutes · soaking time about 30 minutes

Grilled Fruit Kebabs with Spiced Yogurt

For the yogurt
2 cups full-fat yogurt
zest of 1 orange
1 tsp ground cardamom
½ tsp ground cinnamon
2 pinches of ground anise
pinch of ground cloves
¾oz (20g) chopped pistachios
1 tbsp sugar, plus extra to taste if needed

For the fruit kebabs
1 small pineapple, peeled, brown eyes
    removed, quartered lengthwise, then cut
    into 4 equal-sized chunks
1 mango, flesh cut into bite-sized chunks
2 apricots, pitted, quartered, then each
    quarter halved
1 banana, cut into 1½in (4cm) thick slices

Also
4 wooden skewers (8in/20cm each)

1 Soak the wooden skewers for at least 30 minutes in water. To make the spiced yogurt, mix yogurt with orange zest, cardamom, cinnamon, anise, cloves, pistachios, and sugar in a bowl, stirring until the sugar has dissolved. Add more sugar to taste, if desired.

2 To assemble the fruit kebabs, slide chunks of fruit alternately onto the skewers and grill on the barbecue over low heat for 1 minute each side. Slide the fruit off the kebabs and divide between 4 plates. Serve with the spiced yogurt.

For 4 people
Preparation time about 20 minutes · baking time about 30 minutes

Chocolate Cake Baked in an Orange

3½oz (100g) dark chocolate
1 tbsp cocoa powder
1 cup all-purpose flour
1 tsp baking powder
salt
¾ cup confectioner's sugar
4 oranges, juice reserved
2 tbsp soft butter
1 egg
2–3 drops pure vanilla extract

Also
8 pieces aluminum foil (12 x 12in/
  30 × 30cm each)

1 Finely grate the chocolate. This will be easier if you chill the chocolate for a while first. Combine the grated chocolate with the cocoa powder, flour, baking powder, a pinch of salt, and confectioner's sugar. The flour mixture can be prepared at home up to this point and stored in a container. The next steps can be continued at the campsite kitchen.

2 Slice a lid in the top quarter of the oranges. Hollow out the oranges with a spoon. Squeeze the pulp between your hands and measure out 1 cup orange juice. Put the flour mixture into a bowl or pan. Add the orange juice, butter, egg, and pure vanilla extract and stir with a wooden spoon until you have a smooth consistency.

3 Fill the hollowed-out oranges two-thirds full with the mixture and place the lids on to close. Wrap each one in 2 pieces of aluminum foil. Place on the barbecue and bake the cakes for about 30 minutes. Remove and let cool for 10 minutes, then unwrap the foil and serve.

Campfire version
The oranges can be put directly into the embers of a campfire and cooked there. You may need to shorten or lengthen the cooking time, depending on how hot the embers are in the fire or on the barbecue. Ideally test the cakes with a skewer after about 20 minutes. If an inserted wooden skewer comes out with cake mixture on it, continue baking for another 5 minutes before testing again. The cake is cooked when the skewer comes out clean.

Ingredient packing list: Essential supplies

Which pantry foods are absolutely essential for your travels? And what else could you pack if you have the room? Here is a list of travel basics and nice-to-have ingredients, which we suggest for making our recipes.

Basics

· maple syrup/honey
· baking powder
· Dijon/other mustard
· canned tomatoes/tomato puree
· vinegar
· drinks (water, lemonade, alcoholic beverages)
· instant stock powder or cubes
· coffee/tea
· garlic
· flour
· pasta
· oil
· pepper
· salt
· sugar
· onions

Nice to have

· couscous
· cocoa powder
· cans (such as beans, corn, and chickpeas)
· jam/chocolate hazelnut spread
· mie noodles
· nuts (including almonds) and seeds (such as sunflower seeds, cashews, and sesame seeds)
· confectioner's sugar
· risotto rice
· soy sauce
· corn starch
· dried fruit (such as cranberries and apricots)
· dried yeast
· white bread crumbs
· favorite spices and herbs (such as nutmeg, chili powder, rosemary, oregano)

Equipment packing list that campers swear by

There are certain things nobody should be without in their mobile kitchen, such as a good knife, and then there are the luxury items–the things you could do without, but which make life just a little bit easier.

Basic kitchen equipment

· aluminum foil
· mugs/glasses/cups/plates (possibly camping cooking set)
· utensils (knives, forks, tablespoons, and teaspoons)
· freezer bags (resealable)
· kitchen towels
· wooden skewers
· wooden spoon
· corkscrew and can opener
· paper towels
· measuring cup
· knives (2 x chef's knives, 2 x vegetable knives)
· garbage bags
· frying pan (large, with lid)
· chopping board
· bowls (plus dishwashing bowl if room)
· colander
· potato peeler
· dishwashing liquid and sponges
· saucepans (no plastic handles, with lids)

Still have room to spare?

· espresso pot
· bamboo paddle skewers
· barbecue tongs
· garlic press
· kitchen twine
· spatula/fish slice
· grater (for vegetables and cheese)
· scissors
· balloon whisk
· silicone basting brush
· tablecloth

Don't forget:
For the recipes in this book, you'll need measuring cups with at least a 1 cup capacity.

Index

Penguin
Random
House

For DK UK

Translator Alison Tunley
Editor Claire Cross
Senior Editor Kate Meeker
US Editors Jenny Wilson, Jennette ElNaggar
Editorial Assistant Poppy Blakiston Houston
Senior Art Editor Glenda Fisher
Jacket Designer Harriet Yeomans
Producer, Pre-production Heather Blagden
Senior Producer Igrain Roberts
Managing Editor Stephanie Farrow
Managing Art Editor Christine Keilty

For DK Germany

Publisher Monika Schlitzer
Managing Editor Caren Hummel
Project Manager Anne Heinel, Melanie Haizmann
Production Dorothee Whittaker
Production Coordinator Arnika Marx
Producer Jenny Kolbe

First American Edition, 2019
Published in the United States by DK Publishing
1450 Broadway, 8th Floor, New York 10018

A catalog record for this book is available
from the Library of Congress.
ISBN: 978-1-4654-8396-6

DK books are available at special discounts when purchased in
bulk for sales promotions, premiums, fund-raising, or educational
use. For details, contact DK Publishing Special Markets, 345
Hudson St., New York, New York 10014 or SpecialSales@dk.com.

Printed and bound in China

A WORLD OF IDEAS:
SEE ALL THERE IS TO KNOW

www.dk.com